Studies in the
Pastoral Epistles

STUDIES
IN THE PASTORAL
EPISTLES

Anthony Tyrrell Hanson

*Professor of Theology, University of Hull
and Examining Chaplain to the Archbishop of York*

LONDON

S·P·C·K

1968

First published in 1968
by S.P.C.K.
Holy Trinity Church
Marylebone Road
London N.W.1

Printed in Great Britain by
The Camelot Press Ltd., London and Southampton

SBN 281 02258 5

Contents

Abbreviations

Texts

The Hebrew Bible is cited from R. Kittel, *Biblia Hebraica*, 4th edn (Stuttgart 1949)

The Greek Bible is cited from A. Rahlfs, *Septuaginta*, 4th edn (Stuttgart 1950)

The Greek New Testament is cited from K. Aland, M. Black, B. M. Metzger, and A. Wikgren, *The Greek New Testament* (Stuttgart 1966)

The English Bible is cited from the *Revised Standard Version* (London 1952 edn)

Introduction

As far as concerns scholarship in English at least, the study of the
Pastoral Epistles has been polarized by the question of Pauline
authorship. Ever since the publication of P. N. Harrison's *The
Problem of the Pastoral Epistles* in 1921, almost all serious works on
the Pastoral Epistles published in English have been largely
concerned with the question of authorship. The one exception,
perhaps, is Sir R. Falconer's *The Pastoral Epistles* (Oxford 1937),
but one gains the impression that he never had the time to produce
the really important work on the Pastoral Epistles that he might
have done. This polarization was no doubt inevitable: one cannot
study the Pastoral Epistles without encountering the question of
authorship. One cannot suspend one's judgement about it,
though some have apparently attempted this. W. Lock in the
International Critical Commentary gave the impression of being
unable to make up his mind; but his Commentary is not the
better for this. Unfortunately, many of those who (quite rightly)
made up their minds on the question of authorship have devoted
an undue amount of space in their commentaries to vindicating
their decision. This has meant that some of the most interesting
and difficult passages in the Pastoral Epistles have not received
the attention they deserved.

In Germany one would have said that the question had been
decided against the Pauline authorship, except for the publication of J. Jeremias' Commentary in 1963, in which he defends the
Pauline authorship of the entire Epistles (leaning fairly heavily,
it must be added, on the secretary hypothesis). Jeremias in his
turn owes some of his arguments to an unpublished doctoral
thesis of Wm Nauck (it is much to be desired that it should be
published). Nauck, while ostensibly remaining neutral on the
question of authorship, emphasizes so much the Jewish rather than

the Hellenistic background of the Pastorals, that one suspects him of intending to prepare the way for a vindication of the Pauline authorship. Although his arguments fall very far short of proof or even very great conviction, his work has the merit of attempting to begin from the text of the Pastorals itself, without first deciding the question of authorship.

In the meantime we have the exhaustive commentary of M. Dibelius, revised by Hans Conzelmann in 1955. For information about the literary and religious background of the Pastorals this must remain an indispensable work for many years to come. The authors reject Pauline authorship altogether. On very similar lines, though written at a more popular level, is B. S. Easton's Commentary of 1948; its only drawback perhaps is a tendency to press the evidence in favour of a date which would make the author of the Pastorals a contemporary of Marcion. C. Spicq in his Commentary of 1947 supplies a wealth of information, both historical and literary. Though he writes from a somewhat *parti pris* position, he is frequently a good antidote against the sceptical tendency of Dibelius-Conzelmann. We have recently had two excellent commentaries in English, both aiming roughly at the undergraduate level, one on each side of the debate. Despite the valuable insights which J. N. D. Kelly frequently provides, C. K. Barrett seems to have the better of the argument as far as the question of authorship is concerned. Neither Jeremias nor Kelly has really moved the balance of probability, which still remains, in my view, strongly against Pauline authorship.

These studies originated in my being asked to write the Cambridge Bible Commentary on the Pastorals. This is a series designed for the higher forms of schools, and so did not involve the discussion of many points of scholarship. But as I went through the Epistles, I marked several places where I felt that the commentators had not provided very much light, places about which I thought I would like to inquire further. In some instances ideas occurred to me which did not seem to have been tried out by anyone else, and I was anxious to explore them. When I had finished the Commentary, therefore, I turned to the further exploration of these passages. This is why at some points I have reached conclusions in these studies which differ from my opinions expressed in the Commentary. At first my purpose was to write one or two articles for scholarly journals, but as I proceeded I found so much material which required to be included that the articles have turned into a book. This approach may, therefore, claim the merit of beginning from the text of the Pastoral Epistles and attempting to pursue the argument from that point. Instead of asking, "Could Paul have written such and such a passage?", I have tried to ask, "What does this passage mean? What is its significance? Why is it cast in that form?" So these studies are not designed to prove anything about the Pauline authorship. They are an attempt to examine certain passages in the Pastoral Epistles on their own merits.

At the same time, it would be affectation to suppose that complete impartiality and suspension of judgement on the question of authorship is possible. Though my primary aim was not connected with the question of authorship, I did begin with certain convictions on the subject, convictions which, I should say, have not been altered by my studies. I believed that the great bulk of the Epistles was not written by Paul, but by someone else living about forty years later. About twenty verses in all, mostly in 2 Timothy 4, I believed to constitute genuinely Pauline fragments, but, as I do not deal with any of these verses in the studies found in this book, to all intents and purposes I treat the Pastoral Epistles as non-Pauline. They were written, I believe, about the year A.D. 105, probably in Asia Minor. They were all written by the one author, and I do not find sufficient evidence to suggest in what order they were written. My reasons for reaching these conclusions I have set forth in my Commentary, published in 1966. The dating seems to me to be fixed by Acts and 1 Clement on the one hand, with both of which the author seems to have had acquaintance, and on the other by Polycarp's letter to the Philippians, which undoubtedly quotes the Pastorals. But there is some reason to believe that the section which quotes them was written as late as 135, so we do not seem to have a very clear *terminus ante quem.* The absence of references to persecution in the Pastorals, and the similarity in situation to what we find in the Johannine Epistles, inclines one to put them before rather than after Pliny's governship of Bithynia and the Letters of Ignatius. Hence the approximate date of 105.

The order of the eight studies does not follow the order of the Epistles. The first two studies belong to the same passage; they come first because it was the absence of light in the commentaries on that strange phrase *hedraiōma tēs alētheias* that first set me off on my researches. The next four studies (3–6) all originated in mere question marks which I set against this or that verse as I went through the Epistles. In every case much more proved to be behind the passage in question than I had originally suspected. The last two studies are liturgical and were already partly formed in my mind when I wrote the commentary.

These studies will have been justified in my eyes if they serve to show how much of value is to be found in the Pastoral Epistles when one studies them for their own sake.

I

The Foundation of Truth:
1 Timothy 3.15

You may know how one ought to behave in the household of God, which is the church of the living God, the pillar and bulwark of the truth

We begin by examining that word translated "bulwark" in the RSV, *hedraiōma*. The older English versions prefer the translation "ground", though they both (AV and RV) offer "stay" in the margin. The moderns tend to prefer "bulwark" (NEB, Moffatt). But Phillips and Monsignor Knox both translate the word "foundation".[1] The great F. J. A. Hort has written: "There is no clear evidence that *hedraiōma* ever means 'ground', it is rather 'firmamentum', a stay or bulwark."[2] The difficulty is that there is no evidence at all as to what the word meant before its occurrence in 1 Timothy 3.15, since this is its first appearance in Greek literature. It occurs in a context that looks like a quotation. All scholars are agreed that verse 16 is a quotation from an early Christian hymn, and the previous verse with its triple designation of the Church as "household (or house) of God", "pillar", and "*hedraiōma* of the truth", has a liturgical ring about it, though it does not follow, of course, that it is a quotation from the same source as provided the ensuing verse. We are justified, therefore, in looking for antecedents to *hedraiōma* in Jewish-Christian literature.

It is Spicq who has provided the clue. He points out that there is a word ἕδρασμα which occurs in some Greek translations of 1 Kings 8.13,[3] though he does not elaborate this point. In fact verse 13 does not appear in the LXX, but it is inserted as verse 53a.

The Hebrew of 8.13b is *mākhōn lᵉshibhtᵉkhāʿōlāmim* "a place for thee to dwell in for ever". When the LXX translates this phrase in 3 Kingdoms 8.53a, it offers τοῦ κατοικεῖν ἐπὶ καινότητος, This last word is certainly a mistranslation, though how it originated is by no means clear.[4] The point is, however, that certain Greek versions offer a translation ἕδρασμα τῇ καθέδρᾳ (or τῆς καθέδρας) at 3 Kingdoms 8.13. These are the LXX of Codex Coislinianus, and one other Greek minuscule. It is also found in Origen's recension and in some versions of Lucian's. The same Hebrew phrase *mākhōn lᵉshibhtᵉkhā* is translated by ἕδρασμα τῆς καθέδρας in Symmachus' version of Exodus 15.17. This translation of Exodus 15.17 also occurs in some manuscripts of Philo's citation of it in *De plantatione Noe* 47.[5] Though Symmachus himself lived in the second half of the second century, recent research has shown that his version was based on earlier translations of the Old Testament into Greek which were current in the first and second centuries.[6]

There is also evidence in the Vulgate to support the view that *mākhōn lᵉshibhtᵉkhā* was taken to mean "foundation" in early Christian circles. The Vulgate translation of this phrase in 3 Regum 8.13 is *firmissimum solium tuum in sempiternum*.[7] If this is a direct rendering of the Hebrew, then *mākhōn* is taken as an adjective and *shebheth* is taken to mean "foundation" rather than "habitation". Certainly it owes nothing to the LXX κατοικεῖν ἐπὶ καινότητος. It is nearer the sense of *hedrasma*. In 3 Regum 8.43 the same Hebrew phrase is rendered *in firmamento habitaculi tui* and in 8.49 as *in firmamento solii tui*, but only a few verses earlier, in 8.39, we find *in loco habitationis tuae*. What all this goes to show is that *mākhōn* could be rendered as *firmamentum* and that *firmamentum* in this context could not possibly mean "prop or stay". It must mean "firm ground", "foundation", or, most likely of all, simply "firmament". This is made quite certain by the translation of the Hebrew word *rāqīaʿ* in Genesis 1.7 f. It is regularly translated as *firmamentum*. The Vulgate, therefore, supplies a most remarkable link between *hedrasma* in 1 Kings 8.15 and *hedraiōma* in 1 Timothy 3.15, since the Vulgate translation of this last verse is *columna et firmamentum veritatis*. We are thus in a position to question very definitely Hort's confident assertion that *hedraiōma* cannot mean "foundation". On the contrary, any Old Testament antecedents that can be found for the word point in exactly that direction, and that is undoubtedly the meaning that is intended by the Vulgate translation. H. von Soden was therefore justified when he paraphrased the word in 1 Timothy 3.15 as *das Festlegete*[8] and drew attention to the use of *themelios* in 2 Timothy 2.19. This last is a passage which we examine later on. For the moment it is sufficient to cite Colossians 1.23, where Christians are urged to be τῇ πίστει τεθεμελιωμένοι καὶ ἕδραιοι, "grounded and firmly established in the faith"; the two roots are used together and explain each other.

Now that we have given good grounds for connecting *hedraiōma* in 1 Timothy 3.15 with 1 Kings 8.13, a whole set of other correspondences between the two passages is lighted up. The author of 1 Timothy writes of the *house of God*, the *pillar* and *foundation* of the truth. All three phrases can be found, either explicitly or implicitly, in 1 Kings 8.10–13: in verse 11 we read "the glory of the Lord filled the house of the Lord". Here then is the house of God. But in verse 10 this glory is identified with the cloud: "when the priests came out of the holy place, a cloud filled the house of the Lord". This cloud is, of course, the *Sheᵏīnāh*, the visible sign of God's presence, and we are not surprised to learn that the Targum paraphrases 1 Kings 8.13 thus: "Adonai has been pleased to establish his *Sheᵏīnāh* in Jerusalem."[9] But this cloud is identical with the pillar of cloud in the wilderness. In Exodus 33.9 we read: "When Moses entered the tent, the pillar of cloud would descend and stand at the door of the tent, and the Lord would speak with Moses." Similarly, in Numbers 12.5 the pillar of cloud descends when the Lord is about to adjudicate between Moses, Aaron, and Miriam. And in Deuteronomy 31.15, when Joshua is about to be appointed as Moses' successor, "the Lord appeared in the tent in a pillar of cloud; and the pillar of cloud stood by the door of the tent". The significance, therefore, of the cloud which fills the newly consecrated temple in 1 Kings 8.10–11 is to show that the pillar of cloud, which formerly visited the tabernacle, is now permanently established in the temple. A careful study of 1 Corinthians 10.1–11 suggests that in St Paul's thought the pre-existent Christ was present with the Israelites not only in the smitten rock but also in the pillar of cloud that led them across the Red Sea.[10] Thus, when we compare 1 Timothy 3.15 with 1 Kings 8.10–13, we find that there are no fewer than three connecting links, house, pillar, and foundation, all of which could lend themselves to a christological interpretation by early Christians.

That this is not merely a coincidence is made very likely by the fact that we can find in the New Testament a vein of speculation about the relationship of Christ to Solomon's temple. This is, of course, the general theme of the Epistle to the Hebrews, but it is brought to a much more explicit expression in Stephen's speech in Acts 7. It is surely very difficult to deny a close connection between this speech and the Epistle to the Hebrews, so the fact that our theme is found in both is also significant. Stephen pursues his outline history of Israel up to the building of the temple by Solomon, and then in 7.48 breaks off with the assertion, backed by prophetic testimony, that God does not dwell in houses made with hands. I have argued in *Jesus Christ in the Old Testament*[11] that throughout his speech Stephen is ambiguously referring to the pre-existent Christ. It is the pre-existent Christ who appeared to Moses as the angel in the burning bush, and so on. It is even likely that R. P. C. Hanson's conjecture is correct, that "Jesus" in 7.45 is deliberately ambiguous.[12] It was not only Joshua but also the pre-existent Jesus who was present with Israel in the occupation of Canaan. In verse 46 David is described as asking "leave to find a habitation [*skēnōma*] for the house of Jacob". But it was Solomon who built a house for him. There is a deliberate contrast between *skēnōma* and *oikos* (house) and behind the passage lies Psalm 132 (131 in LXX). The phrase "a habitation for the house of Jacob" is a quotation from Psalm 132.5, with "house" substituted for "God". Kirsopp Lake and H. J. Cadbury, rightly no doubt, defend this reading.[13] But they say it means "David wished to build a habitation (of God) for the house of Jacob". This is surely to miss the point: Stephen is arguing that the Christ always was the true house of God, and also became the true heir of the house of Jacob. By substituting "house" for "God" in the Psalm quotation he is therefore killing two birds with one stone: he is suggesting that he for whom the house was actually built was not *Theos* (i.e. the Father) but the Son, the pre-existent Christ who appeared to Moses in the tabernacle. And he is also claiming that this Son became, through his incarnation, the true house of Jacob. Moreover, we can trace the influence of Psalm 132 further in this passage. In the Psalm David swears that he will not sleep till he has found "a place for the Lord [τόπον τῷ κυρίῳ], a habitation for the God of Jacob", and in verse 10 he prays: "Turn not away the presence of thine anointed [τοῦ χριστοῦ σου]." This would certainly speak to an early Christian of the Messiah. Finally, in verse 14 comes God's acceptance of Jerusalem as his dwelling-place:

This is my dwelling [*katapausis*] for ever and ever.[14]

Both *topos* and *katapausis* are taken up in the Isaiah quotation in 7.49, where the prophet asks: τίς τόπος τῆς καταπαύσεώς μου; "What is the place of my rest?" The answer that Stephen implies (and the whole speech finds its main significance in what it implies rather than in what it says) is that Christ, the Son, is the place of God's rest. We remember Philo's frequent use of *topos* as a periphrasis for God or the Logos, for example *De Somniis 1.* 61f[15], where he distinguishes a threefold meaning for *topos* in scripture: (*a*) a place in space, (*b*) the Logos, and (*c*) God himself.[16] The conclusion at which Stephen wishes his hearers to arrive is that the only place where God is really to be met is the Son, the true temple or house of God, and that therefore Solomon was wrong to build a house for God. Here then we have a New Testament passage that is vitally concerned with the Christian understanding of 1 Kings 8.10–13.

This is not a conclusion with which all scholars would agree. There are those, of course, like Foakes-Jackson, who totally fail to see any Christian content in Stephen's speech: "In the entire speech of Stephen the name of Jesus is never mentioned and there is no allusion to a Messiah."[17] In fact, the anointed, the Messiah is referred to twice in that Psalm quoted by Stephen (Ps. 132.10 and 17), and there may be even an ambiguous reference to Jesus in verse 45, as we have noted. But others, who would allow a rather more Christian content to the speech, deny that the condemnation of the temple has any connection with Christology. For example, Marcel Simon writes: "It seems that his condemnation of the Temple is quite independent of Christ's coming."[18] Simon would connect Stephen with one tradition in the Greek-speaking Diaspora which was opposed on spiritual grounds to the localized cult. He suggests that there is a distinction in septuagintal usage between *katoikein* and *skēnōma*, the former being used for God's permanent dwelling in heaven, and the latter for his temporary sojourn in the sanctuary, and he repeats Foakes-Jackson's statement that there is no distinctively Christian message in the speech. The same distinction between *katoikein* and *skēnōma* in the LXX is made by L. W. Barnard,[19] so we might consider this first: surely the LXX of 2 Kingdoms 8.53a, a translation of the MT of 1 Kings 8.12–13, is sufficient to disprove the absoluteness of this assertion. The verse runs in the LXX:

> The Lord has known the sun in the heavens[20]
> He said he would dwell [*katoikein*] in darkness.
> Build my house, a splendid house for thyself,
> To dwell in in newness.

The LXX translation is astray in at least three places here (see p. 121, n. 4) but it is quite plain that *katoikein* must indicate the mode in which God dwells in the temple in at least one of its two occurrences here. Simon seems to have misunderstood Stephen's intended meaning when he says that the temple is not connected with Christ's coming. It is the pre-existent Christ who is referred to throughout, hence the ending of the tabernacle and the setting up of the temple could be regarded as having a direct relation to Christ. Thus Simon's conclusion (op. cit., p. 141), "Stephen's

Christology seems to be of a very primitive and archaic type", can hardly stand. Stephen's Christology, as far as we can make it out, was very like that of the author of the Epistle to the Hebrews, and Barnard's attempt to distinguish between the two types of theology is misdirected. By divorcing Stephen's speech from Hebrews, he would try to emphasize the link between Acts 7 and the Epistle of Barnabas. The gap between Stephen and Barnabas is well illustrated by *Ep. Barnabas* 16.10 where Isaiah 66.1 is quoted, and the author says that the temple of God is already built, it is the temple in our hearts, and he does not mention the Church in this connection. His conclusion is: "This [*sc.* Christ in us] is the spiritual temple built to the Lord."[21] Stephen insists that Christ is the true temple, Barnabas that our hearts are the true temple. In fact the three works are in the same tradition, though the Epistle of Barnabas is distinctly later in the tradition.

Much more convincing are those scholars who emphasize the link between Stephen's speech and Hebrews. Of these is Oscar Cullman, who claims that according to Stephen the supreme act of disobedience on the part of the Jews was the building of Solomon's temple.[22] He finds evidence for the existence of a group of early Christian "Hellenists" who rejected the temple cult, and he would connect this with all the references in all four Gospels to "Destroy this temple". He believes that this tradition goes back to Jesus himself. He traces this tradition not only in Stephen's speech and the Synoptic Gospels, but more particularly in the Fourth Gospel, in such passages as John 4.20–4. He would agree that the use of *skēnōma* and cognates implies that Jesus is the true tabernacle, and he considers that in the Epistle to the Hebrews the concept of the Christian community as the true temple is fundamental. Finally, we may note that in his opinion the Qumran community helped to prepare the way for a total rejection of the temple cult. The reference to the Fourth Gospel and to Qumran is particularly significant in view of the evidence shortly to be reviewed. We might also mention an article by Guy Wagner,[23] in which he brings together Acts 7, Hebrews 8, a number of passages from Revelation (11.19; 21.22–3), and Mark 14.58, in order to show that there is a strong early Christian belief to the effect that earthly temples were no more than "human works doomed to destruction", whereas the new temple is to be the Lord's risen body. Once again the connection between house of God, house of Israel, and Christ is strongly underlined.

But we can point to another passage where Christ is presented as the true tabernacle, John 5.35:

> He [the Baptist] was a burning and shining lamp [ἐκεῖνος ἦν ὁ λύχνος ὁ καιόμενος καὶ φαίνων] and you were willing to rejoice [agalliathēnai] for a while in his light.

It is surprising that commentators have on the whole failed to account for the rather remarkable language of this description of the Baptist's ministry. Why should he be called "*the* burning and shining light" (for that is undoubtedly the sense), and why should that remarkable word *agalliathēnai* be used, which really means "celebrate high festival"? Westcott says: "The definite article . . . simply marks the familiar piece of household furniture (compare Mark 4.21; Luke 11.36) . . . there is no evidence to show that it was given to the herald of the Messiah by tradition."[24] H. J. Holtzmann refers to Ben Sira 48.1:[25]

> Then the prophet Elijah arose like a fire,
> and his word burned like a torch.

The Greek for "torch" here is *lampas*. The Hebrew appears to be "a burning furnace".[26] The suggestion is that John's readers would recognize the allusion to Elijah as a light. This is supported by Blass–Debrunner 243.1,[27] who paraphrases the words in John 5.35 thus: "he who alone really deserves the designation 'light' (cf. Sir. 48.1 (with ὡς) of Elijah)." But is it not expecting a lot of John's readers to recognize a quotation from Ben Sira? Others have therefore preferred to cite 2 Samuel 21.17, where David is described as "the lamp of Israel".[28] This is the reference favoured by Hoskyns.[29] Bultmann has a different way of explaining the definite article: "Der Art. entspricht dem Gleichnisstil, vgl.

Mark 4.21."³⁰ This seems rather a feeble explanation. R. H. Lightfoot would explain the article as pointing forward to the two participles: "It has been suggested that the right translation here is: 'He was the lamp that was kindled and shines', i.e. John's light was derivative, not self-originated."³¹ But this would surely require the perfect participle. C. H. Dodd merely cites a number of objects to which the Rabbis applied the word "light": the Torah, the temple, and even a rabbi contemporary with the author of the Fourth Gospel, Jochanan ben Zakkai.³² C. K. Barrett fails to find any Old Testament source for λύχνος.³³ The phrase "He *was* a burning and a shining light" has also caused difficulty. Most editors suggest it implies that John was already in prison by this point in Jesus' ministry (so Holtzmann, Lagrange,³⁴ Lightfoot).

It is J. H. Bernard, however, who provides the clue to the most satisfactory explanation of this verse, though he does not make any use of it.³⁵ He points out that Psalm 132.17b came to be applied by the Fathers to John the Baptist. This runs: "I have prepared a lantern [λύχνον] for my anointed." In fact John 5.35 is based on Psalm 132, the same Psalm as Stephen quotes in the passage from Acts 7 that we have just been considering. But we must first go back a little in order to explain "the *burning* light". Exodus 27.20–1 runs thus: "And you shall command the people of Israel that they bring to you pure beaten olive oil for the light, that a lamp [LXX λύχνος] may be set up to burn (LXX same verb as "burning" in John 5.35) continually.³⁶ In the tent of meeting, outside the veil which is before the testimony, Aaron and his sons shall tend it from evening to morning before the Lord."

This is the burning light which shines outside the holy of holies in order to show the way there. It is to be within the "tent of meeting", which the LXX translates "tent of witness', but outside the veil. We must remember that John 5.35 forms part of a passage which is much concerned with the witness given to the Son. The author of the Fourth Gospel would see this light as a type of the forerunner: as the light gave witness to the Presence in the holy of holies under the old dispensation, so the Baptist gives witness to the incarnate Presence under the new. The Presence is the same in both dispensations.

We now turn to Psalm 132, with Bernard's useful parallel in mind. The crucial verses are 16–17, which we may translate direct from the LXX:

> Her priests [Zion's] will I clothe with salvation,
> And her saints shall greatly rejoice
> [*agalliasei agalliasontai*];
> There shall I raise up a horn for David,
> I have prepared a lantern for my anointed
> [λύχνον τῷ χριστῷ μου].[37]

We have already pointed out the significance of the previous verses, such as verse 5, with its reference to *topos* and *skēnōma*, and verse 8, with its mention of the Lord's *anapausis* or resting-place. All these details would of course be as significant to John as they would to Stephen.[38] But John has quoted a verse of this Psalm which is not referred to in Acts 7, Psalm 132.17, where the saints "rejoice". This then is the source of that unexpected word *agalliathēnai* in John 5.35. This verse could perhaps be described as a Christian midrash on Psalm 132. John the Baptist is the burning and shining light set outside the holy of holies, to point the way there. This light was promised through David by God, a lantern to guide the way to the Messiah when he should appear in the flesh. Then would be the era of the messianic feast, when all faithful Israel would rejoice as priests in the salvation which God had granted them in the Messiah.[39] The Jews, however, treated the Baptist's ministry as a temporary phenomenon; they rejoiced in his light, but did not advance into the holy of holies as he was directing them. This is his true function, and this perhaps best explains the past tense "He *was* the burning and shining light"; it refers rather to fulfilment of prophecy, or typology, than to the Baptist's imprisonment. If the Jews had only realized it, the Baptist's role was outlined for them in Scripture ever since the days of David.

Here then are two other passages in the New Testament to put beside 1 Timothy 3.15. In both Acts 7.47–50 and John 5.35 we find a Christian treatment of Psalm 132. The point of both is to show that the true sanctuary is Jesus Christ and both imply that it was the pre-existent Christ who was present in the tabernacle of old. What they both have in common with 1 Timothy 3.15 is the belief in Christ as the true tabernacle for God's presence among men, and that behind all three passages lies the Christian interpretation of an Old Testament passage which is so interpreted as to witness to this belief.

Bertil Gärtner has recently found comparable material in the Qumran documents.[40] On pages 66–70 of his book he examines 1 Timothy 3.15. He assumes the Pauline authorship of this passage, a position which we cannot accept, but this does not in any way affect his interpretation of it. He begins by discussing οἶκος Θεοῦ "household of God" in 1 Timothy 3.15, and brings together 2 Corinthians 6.16, where Christians are described as a "temple of the living God", Hebrews 3.1–6, where they are called Christ's house, and 1 Timothy 3.5, where the church is compared to a household. Obviously the thought of the church as God's house easily passes over into that of God's household, since οἶκος can mean either. It seems likely that the author of the Pastorals has in this passage imported the idea of "household" as a link between Christian behaviour ("how to behave in the household of God") and the church as God's house, which is what the midrash he quotes is concerned with. The author is fond of the "household" figure, as is shown both by verse 5 and by 2 Timothy 2.20–1, another passage where he seems to have taken the thought of a building from his source and modified it to mean "household". The citation of Hebrews 3.1–6 is particularly relevant to this passage because there also we have Christ as the house of God in both the old and new dispensations.[41] It is worth noting in this connection that Paul never unambiguously calls the church the house of God, though we do find the building-figure occasionally.

Gärnter next proceeds to offer parallels to *hedraiōma* from the Qumran documents. He assumes without discussion that it means "foundation" and never considers the meaning "prop" at all. His first parallel is from I QS v 5f, which he translates ". . . to lay a foundation of truth for Israel, for the community of the eternal covenant, to make atonement for all those who of their own free will have dedicated themselves [to be] a sanctuary in Aaron and a house of truth in Israel." The phrase "foundation of truth" is *mūsad 'emeth* and "house of truth" is *bēth ha'emeth*. In I QS viii 7f, the members of the community are called "witnesses to the truth". They are also described as a wall and a cornerstone whose foundations shall not be shaken, and "a house of justice and truth in Israel". In I QS ix 3f, the founding of the community is a laying of the "foundation of the holy spirit [*yᵉsōd rūach*]", which is defined as "eternal truth". Gärtner thinks that this truth is the Law. "Truth" could mean either the innermost truth or the in-group that possesses the truth, or both at the same time. Gärtner suggests that in 1 Timothy 3.15 "the truth" means the revelation in Christ, which is no doubt correct. He would link "the mystery of our religion" with this, but we have a fuller discussion of this phrase in the next section. Comparing this verse with 1 Corinthians 3.11, he writes: "There does not seem to be much difference between 1 Timothy 3.15, in which the Church is said to be foundation, and 1 Corinthians 3.11, in which it is Christ who is the foundation, *themelios*." We may conjecture that the difference of terms indicates a difference of authors. Finally Gärtner suggests that "the rare word *hedraiōma* is to be traced back to such Hebrew concepts as *mūsād, sōd*, etc".

These two passages from the Manual of Discipline of the Qumran sect have also been discussed by Otto Betz.[42] He points out that the phrase "foundation of truth" occurs in what is in effect a midrash on Isaiah 28.16, the well-known text about the cornerstone and the sure foundation. The Qumran sectaries understood this cornerstone and foundation as a reference to their own community. Early Christians understood it as Christ primarily, and secondarily as the community in Christ. We have suggested precisely this explanation for the phrase in 1 Timothy 3.15; the *hedraiōma* of truth, we have suggested, is first Christ, the true temple, and secondly the community that lives in him, the Church. This is a relationship which can be paralleled more than once: language which in the Qumran documents is used of the community and its teaching is in Christianity used of the community and its Lord.[43]

Such fantastic claims about the relation between the Qumran community and the origin of Christianity have been seriously advanced in certain quarters recently, that one hesitates to be too dogmatic about claiming any relationship at all between the Qumran documents and the New Testament. But the evidence produced by Gärtner does strongly reinforce the suggestion that the language of 1 Timothy 3.15 has its origin in early Christian Christology and ecclesiology. In Qumran the community could be called "the foundation of truth", even though the Hebrew word is not the same as that on which we have claimed that *hedraiōma* is based. It was quite natural in one Jewish sect to claim that the community is God's house, God's foundation, the house of truth. This is not to suggest that 1 Timothy 3.15 is based on a speculation of the Qumran community. On the contrary there is one all-important difference: the New Testament passage is messianic, or rather christological; the Qumran quotations are not. Moreover, if the interpretation advanced above is correct, the New Testament passage was originally based on a specific part of the Old Testament, 1 Kings 8.10–13. The Qumran passage is based on Isaiah 28.16. But the Qumran quotations show how very easy and natural such speculation would be for early Christians, and they greatly strengthen the case for translating *hedraiōma* as "foundation" rather than "prop", a point upon which so much hangs. And we may also claim that the Qumran parallels help to explain how the house or foundation can be at the same time Christ and the Church.

It is unlikely that the author of the Pastorals had direct access to rabbinic traditions in Hebrew or Aramaic. But this does not mean that the original midrash on 1 Kings 8.10–13 which we have supposed to be behind this passage may not have been in Aramaic. Though on the whole the midrash seems to belong to the tradition of Hebrews and Acts 7, whose authors do not give any signs

of being able to read Hebrew, we must not rule out the possibility that early Christian speculation about the relation of the pre-
existent Christ to the temple may have been in Aramaic. Certainly
the passage from 1 Kings which we have suggested lies behind 1
Timothy 3.15 gave rise to speculations among the Rabbis. 1
Kings 8.13a runs: "I have built thee an exalted house." The phrase
"exalted house" is *bēth z^ebhul* in Hebrew. *Z^ebhul* is a rare word
the meaning of which is not certain and the LXX translator
obviously had difficulty with it because of this. As we have seen,
in the next line occurs the phrase *mākhōn l^eshibht^ekhā*, translated
by RSV "a place for thee to dwell in". Both *z^ebhul* and *mākhōn*
became the subject of rabbinic speculations. In Tractate Hagiga
in the Babylonian Talmud we read of seven heavens, two of
which are named *Z^ebhul* and *Mākhōn* respectively:[44] "Zebul is
that in which [the heavenly] Jerusalem and the Temple and the
Altar are built, and Michael, the great Prince, stands and offers
up therein an offering, for it is said, 'I have surely built thee a
house of habitation (Zebul), a place for thee to dwell in for ever'."
I. Abrahams comments: "The earthly Temple corresponds to
the heavenly sanctuary". The heaven called *Mākhōn* contains
the reserves of snow and so on. Here is speculation very like that
of the early Christians, without the christological element, and
based on 1 Kings 8.13. In Tractate Berakoth we meet an interesting comment on Exodus 15.17, where, as we have observed,
mākhōn occurs, and where some versions translate as *hedrasma*:[45]

> the place, O Lord, which thou hast made for thy abode,
> the sanctuary, O Lord, which thy hands have established.

Rabbi Eliazar said: "Great is the Sanctuary, since it has been
placed between two names, as it is said 'Thou hast made, O Lord,
the sanctuary, O Lord'." We could easily imagine how significant
such a scripture passage would seem to an early Christian, with
his readiness to find in the Old Testament references to a Lord
who was distinct from God.

It is worth pointing out also in this context that there is some
evidence from rabbinic sources for the Christian objection to the

worship of the temple. In Tractate Rosh Hashanah we learn that a certain class of sinners is to be consumed in Gehinnom because "they laid hands on the zebul".[46] Maurice Simon suggests that the reference may be to Jewish Christians because of their repudiation of the temple as the place where true and perfect worship could be offered. If so, this must go back to before the fall of Jerusalem.

To sum up: behind 1 Timothy 3.15, we suggest, lies the work of an early Christian theologian, who originally composed a midrash on 1 Kings 8.10–13. In it he claimed that the true house of God was not the man-made temple erected by Solomon, but the dwelling place indicated in the sacred text was really the Son, the pre-existent Christ, who had manifested his presence in the pillar of cloud, in the divine Sh^{e}kīnāh in the tabernacle, and who is in fact himself the true place, rest, and dwelling of God. No doubt he also believed, though we cannot be sure that he added this to his exegesis, that the Christian Church was the house of God in the new dispensation, the place where the truth was now manifested, where the presence of God in Christ was to be found.

This midrash the author of the Pastorals took over. It does not seem at all likely that he composed it himself. In the rest of his work he does not exhibit a genius equal to such insight, nor does he show much interest in Old Testament exegesis as such. But he does appear to be an excellent man for using and preserving the work of others, and here as in many other places he seems to have incorporated in his epistle this Christian midrash. It would be precarious to speculate as to the form in which the material reached him. Was it in a eucharistic or baptismal prayer? Was it in a hymn or a credal formula? Or as a homily? We do not have enough evidence to be dogmatic about this, as we do not know enough about early Christian forms of worship. It seems likely that he has somewhat altered it in adapting it, either deliberately or because he misunderstood it. In view of the background, 1 Kings 8.10–13, it seems likely that the material was originally christological in intention. The author of the Pastorals has used it in an ecclesiological context. But the difference is not as great as one might imagine: as we have seen, the word *oikos* forms the transitional link. We might guess that the midrash originated in the same sort of circles as produced the Epistle to the Hebrews and Acts 7, whatever those circles were. It was certainly a milieu in which Christian theology of first-rate insight could be produced, but that theology is not, on the whole, Pauline, and this passage may well be considered one more piece of evidence to support the view that Paul is not the author of the Pastoral Epistles.

2

An Academic Phrase:
1 Timothy 3.16a

Great indeed, we confess, is the mystery of our religion.

The interesting word here is that translated "we confess",
homologoumenōs.[1] It carries with it a suggestion of an adversative,
and English translators certainly render it as if it was a very
argumentative word: "without controversy", RV; "beyond all
question", NEB; "No one can deny that", Phillips; "No question
of it", Knox. It is a philosophical word and in Stoicism can
express the thought of living *conformably* to nature, like Horace's

vivere naturae si convenienter oportet.

It is somewhat strange here, because nobody seems to have been
arguing. We pass from what seems to have been a midrash,
whether in the form of prayer, praise, or homily, to what is
undoubtedly a hymn or confession. *Homologoumenōs* makes sense
either in a philosophic or an argumentative contest. We seem
to have neither here. Why is it used?

Some editors have tried to read a confessional source into it.
Thus A. R. C. Leaney translates it "we confess"[2] and the editor
in the *Interpreter's Bible* renders it "we confess and declare in
public",[3] but this seems to be reading a great deal into one word.
The clue to this mystery is, I believe, to be found in the Fourth
Book of Maccabees. This is a rhetorical piece on the subject of the
martyrdom of the seven sons in the Antiochene persecution,
composed apparently about the beginning of the Christian era.[4]
Townshend describes its subject as "the power of ὁ εὐσέβης

λογισμός, the Inspired Reason, to control the passions".[5] Now this remarkable word *homologoumenōs* occurs no fewer than three times in this treatise, always in connection with an enunciation of the theme of the work. Thus in 4 Maccabees 6.31 we read ὁμολογουμένως οὖν δεσπότης τῶν παθῶν ἐστιν ὁ εὐσέβης λογισμός. This we may translate: "Rational piety is thus demonstrably the master of the passions." The same phrase recurs in 7.16 and 16.1. with *hēgemōn* ("leader") and *autokratōr* ("lord") substituted for *despotēs* in the two passages respectively. The author of 4 Maccabees used the word *homologoumenōs*, we may surmise, because it was a word he found in the Stoic writings which he admired, and because he is arguing a case. In each passage he uses it to draw a moral from the courageous behaviour of the martyrs. It is not unfair to conjecture also that he liked the sound of a good philosophic adverb like *homologoumenōs*; it gave an academic air to a work which has some pretensions to being a philosophic treatise. It is indeed an academic word, one which, we feel, would sound well on the Third Programme. It would seem that "demonstrably" would be the translation that conveys best its overtones of nice academic argument.

The author of the Pastorals has lifted this word from 4 Maccabees. This is strongly indicated by the fact that he uses it in a context of "piety", *eusebeia*, also. We have noted above that the author is not much interested in expounding the Old Testament, but he is a keen reader of some of the Jewish apocryphal works, as we shall be showing presently. He certainly did not find *homologoumenōs* in the LXX, for it does not occur there. But he would encounter it in a prominent position in 4 Maccabees, a book with which he was surely familiar. It would strike him as a good word, a useful one with which to adorn a sentence that must act as a transition between two sets of material which he wishes to quote. It would give an academic air to his Epistle, and we are not far wrong in suggesting that the philosophic level of 4 Maccabees is just about as deep into philosophy as our author would be able to go without finding himself out of his depth. It is true indeed that in the context in which he uses the word it functions neither as an adversative nor as a pointer to a philosophical truth. But that would not matter from his point of view, it would serve his purpose. His master in moral philosophy had repeatedly written that "rational piety is demonstrably master of the passions". He would assert that "the mystery of piety is demonstrably great". It sounds like moral philosophy. Thus we must dissent from O. Michel's conclusion that the author of Pastorals uses the word quite differently from the way it is used in 4 Maccabees and Josephus.[6] He is, we maintain, deliberately copying 4 Maccabees.[7]

One of the points in which the Pastoral Letters differ most markedly from the acknowledged Pauline Letters is in their use of *eusebeia* and *eusebēs*. Of the four cognates *eusebeia*, *eusebein*, *eusebēs*, and *eusebōs*, not one occurs anywhere in the New Testament except in Acts, 2 Peter, and the Pastoral Epistles. Indeed the whole concept of *eusebeia* is foreign to Paul's theology. *Eusebeia* occurs ten times in the Pastorals, *eusebein* once, and *eusebōs* once. The noun is a favourite one of the author of the Pastorals, and exactly the same can be said of the author of 4 Maccabees. Of the fifty-nine occurrences of the word in the LXX, no fewer than forty-seven come from 4 Maccabees. W. Foerster has recently pointed out that the concept of *eusebeia* is peculiar to the Pastorals and 2 Peter,[8] in the New Testament. It is thought of as a virtue and is quite opposed to the usage of the rest of the New Testament, where *pistis*, *elpis*, and *agapē* are "not virtues in the Greek sense". But the author of 4 Maccabees certainly does believe in the practice of virtues in the Greek sense, and it is from him, we may suggest, that the author of the Pastorals gained his concept of *eusebeia*. D-C is no doubt right when he maintains "the mystery of *eusebeia*" in 3.16a is really no different from "the mystery of the faith" in 3.9.[9] He uses the word "mystery" perhaps because it is undoubtedly a Pauline word; put with *eusebeia* it may serve to suggest both doctrine and praxis.

It may be taken as established, therefore, that the author of the Pastorals was a reader of Maccabees. But there is more evidence besides this that he was a reader of the Maccabean literature. A study of his vocabulary points strongly in this direction; we may take a very small example to begin with, that word in Titus 2.3 translated by RSV "reverent", *hieroprepeis*, literally "like priestesses", so that perhaps a more accurate translation would be "reverend"! It is a fine word, hinting at a natural priesthood of mothers. In the entire LXX it occurs only twice, both occurrences in 4 Maccabees. Next we can cite "youthful passions" in 2 Timothy 2.22, where *neōterikos* "youthful" occurs in the LXX only in 3 Maccabees 4.8, "youthful ease". Then come two words *athanasia* in 1 Timothy 6.16 and *aphtharsia* in 2 Timothy 1.10, both translated by the one word "immortality" in RSV. Of these the first occurs five times in the Book of Wisdom and once in 4 Maccabees and not at all in the rest of the LXX; and the second occurs twice in Wisdom and twice in 4 Maccabees, but nowhere else in the LXX. It might be argued that there is no word in Hebrew for "immortality", and that this is why it does not occur in the Old Testament, but this in itself is a clear indication of the sphere of thought in which the author of the Pastorals moved. He was much more at home in Hellenized Judaism than in the Old Testament proper. Another interesting word is *dunastēs*, which the author of the Pastorals uses for God in 1 Timothy 6.15, translated "Sovereign". It is used nowhere else in the New Testament for God, and nowhere for God in the LXX except in the Books of the Maccabees, where it is so used ten times, and once in Ben Sira 46.5, where the Hebrew is *'El 'Elyon*.[10] A significant word is *philarguria* in 1 Timothy 6.10 "love of money". It is unique in the New Testament and the LXX except for 4 Maccabees 1.26 and 2.15.[11] In both places it occurs in an ethical passage which is much concerned with a discussion of the desirable virtues and reprehensible vices. It seems very likely that it is from here that the author of the Pastorals borrowed the word, in order to coin what is surely one of his least Pauline sentiments.[12] It may be that the difficult phrase in 2 Timothy 2.15 is inspired by a sentence from 4 Maccabees. The phrase is translated by RSV "rightly handling the word of truth": ὀρθοτομοῦντα τὸν λόγον τῆς ἀληθείας. A sentence occurs in 4 Maccabees 1.15: "Rational behaviour may therefore be defined as intelligence with right reason, deliberately choosing the life of wisdom".[13] There does not seem to be much in common in English, but the two passages in Greek share *orthos* and *logos*, and both are in some sense an attempt to describe the good life. The relationship is, it must be admitted, rather distant.

Outside the Books of the Maccabees, the author of the Pastorals certainly knew the Book of Tobit, for he quotes Tobit 4.9 in 1 Timothy 6.19. He may have read the Book of Wisdom, though the two words *athanasia* and *aphtharsia* probably came to him through liturgical sources. A word that poses a very interesting question is *anoia* "folly", which he uses in 2 Timothy 3.9. It is a very much loaded word, indicating mad and senseless behaviour such as one would only attribute to those whose principles of action one considered utterly mistaken. It is used elsewhere in the New Testament only in Luke 6.11 of the behaviour of Jesus' opponents, the scribes and Pharisees. It is used four times in 2 Maccabees to describe the behaviour of the enemies of faithful Israel.[14] It is used in 3 Maccabees by a Ptolemaic monarch to describe what he regards as the fanaticism of the Jews.[15] An interesting question arises from the fact that it occurs twice in the Book of Wisdom: in 15.18 it appears to be used of the witlessness of the animals worshipped by the Egyptians, thereby reflecting the witlessness of the Egyptians themselves. In 19.3 it is used of the foolish behaviour of the Egyptians in pursuing the very Israelites whom they had only recently implored to leave them.[16]

It is with Wisdom 15.18 that we are concerned, because it bears a certain resemblance to 2 Timothy 3.7–9. In this passage the author of the Pastorals is referring to certain heretical teachers, "who will listen to anybody and can never arrive at a knowledge of the truth". He then compares them to Jannes and Jambres, who opposed Moses, and ends with the comment: "but they will not get very far, for their folly [*anoia*] will be plain to all, as was that of those two men." What these two passages, Wisdom 15.18 —16.1 and 2 Timothy 3.7–9, have in common is a background of Jewish speculation about the plagues of Egypt, and the use of the word *anoia* to describe the behaviour of the opponents of Israel at that time. The question is: Can we assume any common source of information?

It may be as well just to say something about Jannes and Jambres. They are two figures of Jewish midrash, identified with the magicians of Pharaoh who withstood Moses. Rabbinic legend also said that they suggested to Pharaoh the plan of killing the Hebrew boy babies, and even identified them with the two young men who accompanied Balaam in Numbers 22.22. In the Talmud they are called Johana and Mamre, and indeed some manuscripts read "Mamres" for "Jambres" in 2 Timothy 3.8.[17] It seems very likely that "Mamre" is the older form of the name, and that it was originally a title belonging to Jannes meaning "the apostate" or "the opponent" from the Hebrew *mārāh*. In the Babylonian Talmud Johana and Mamre are not very formidable figures; indeed in one story they appear more as comedians than villains, for they taunt Moses with carrying coals to Newcastle, on the grounds that in executing the plagues he was bringing magic to Egypt, the home of magic. He replies mildly enough that one must sell one's wares in the best market.[18] Another tradition associates the two magicians with the incident of the Golden Calf, when they instigated the people to rebel against Moses.[19]

But these Talmudic references all come from a time distinctly later than the Pastorals. A much more nearly contemporary reference, and probably the earliest extant, occurs in the Zadokite Fragment. R. H. Charles translates it thus: "For aforetime arose Moses and Aaron through the prince of the lights. But Belial raised Jochannah and his brother with his evil device when the former delivered Israel."[20] The two magicians are also mentioned in Pliny and Apuleius. It seems likely that by the time the Pastorals were written Jannes and Jambres were thought of as appearing only during the period of the plagues, and their main activity consisted in opposing Moses. It is not easy to say in what exactly their folly consisted, according to the author of the Pastorals. Was it shown up by the fact that they confessed themselves unable to turn the dust into gnats, as Moses had done? This incident is narrated in Exodus 8.18–19 and there the magicians explain "This is the finger of God". If so, there may be some sort of connection with Wisdom 15.18—16.1. The author of Wisdom suggests that the plague of vermin was an appropriate punishment for the Egyptians who worshipped vermin, and implies that both vermin and idolaters are equally convicted of lack of intelligence (*anoia*):

> The enemies of thy people worship even the most hateful animals, which are worse than all others, when judged by their lack of intelligence; and even as animals they are not so beautiful in appearance that one would desire them,
> but they have escaped both the praise of God and his blessing.
> Therefore those men were deservedly punished through those creatures, and were tormented by a multitude of animals.

The difficulty with this suggestion is that we cannot tell for certain what are the "animals" to which the author of Wisdom is referring here. He uses two words, *zōa*, which might refer to any animals whatever, and *knōdala*, which really means "any wild animals", but does seem to be used here to mean "inferior animals, vermin". Gregg thinks the reference is primarily to the fish, the crocodile, and the serpent, all worshipped by the Egyptians.[21] But none of these was used in the plagues. Reider would see it rather as applying to locusts, frogs, and flies.[22] Weber would make it refer only to the frogs,[23] and so also Fichtner.[24]

It seems almost as if the comment in Wisdom follows appropriately on to that in the Pastorals. The magicians were shown up as senseless by the fact that, having undertaken to rival Moses, they failed to do so when they failed to manufacture vermin. The whole people of Egypt was then shown up as senseless because they were persecuted by the very senseless creatures that they had senselessly worshipped. What is later in act is earlier in time. If we may date the Book of Wisdom as fairly early in the first century B.C. we may suggest that the midrash had not developed very much by that time at least in the Diaspora. Later a need began to be felt for more definite opponents of Moses, and legend produced

Johana the Opponent. He in his turn developed into Jannes and Jambres, counterparts to Moses and Aaron. This is the stage that has been reached by the time of the Zadokite Fragment (except that the brother is not named) and the Pastoral Epistles. The author of the Pastorals uses the story in order to discountenance his own heretical opponents. Just as the two magicians were unable to compete with Moses when it came to supernatural power, so the author's opponents do not have the power of religion (2 Timothy 3.5.) The conscious connection between the Pastorals and the Book of Wisdom is by no means proved, but both authors were in touch with the same tradition of Jewish Hellenistic midrash, and both no doubt wish to use it for the same purpose, the refutation of their contemporary religious opponents.

3

The Apostates:
2 Timothy 2.19–21

But God's firm foundation stands, bearing this seal: "The Lord knows who are his," and "Let every one who names the name of the Lord depart from iniquity." In a great house there are not only vessels of gold and silver but also of wood and earthenware, and some for noble use, some for ignoble. If any one purifies himself from what is ignoble, then he will be a vessel for noble use, consecrated and useful to the master of the house, ready for any good work.

A foundation which bears a seal consisting of two quotations, apparently from the Old Testament, is a phenomenon which demands some explanation, especially when it occurs in the Pastoral Epistles, whose author is not notably given to exposition of the Old Testament. There is a passage in Paul's Letter to the Romans which is certainly one of the sources of inspiration for these verses; this is Romans 9.14–33. From this is taken the reference to "vessels". Indeed, the phrase "vessels for noble and ignoble use" is actually quoted from Romans 9.21. Paul and the author of the Pastorals are dealing with the same theme, human destiny in the light of God's providence. It seems very likely in addition that the author of the Pastorals has been influenced by a passage from the Book of Wisdom, a suggestion which gains significance in view of our discussion in the last section. The passage is Wisdom 15.7:

> For when a potter treads the soft earth
> and laboriously moulds each vessel for our service,
> he fashions out of the same clay

> both the vessels that serve clean uses,
> and those for contrary uses, making all in like manner;
> but which shall be the use of each of these
> the worker in clay decides.

The author of the Pastorals has taken from Wisdom the thought of some vessels being for clean or unclean use.[1]

In order to understand the author's thought here, it is necessary to examine his main source, Romans 9.14-33. A paraphrase of the argument might run like this: "The theme is the faithful remnant. Is God not unjust in choosing one and rejecting another? No, because it is ultimately a question of grace not of merit, of mercy not of justice. God has a right to have mercy on whom he will—and this includes the right to harden the hearts of whom he will. We men can claim no rights before God, both because we are his creatures and because we are his rebellious creatures. God has therefore tolerated the rebellious (who may be thought of as having destined themselves to destruction);[2] in this toleration his power is shown, as his mercy is shown in the vessels of mercy. Now in fact the distinction between those who receive mercy and those who do not coincides almost, but not quite, with the distinction between Jews and believing Gentiles. This distinction is not absolute, because there has always been a faithful remnant among the Jews themselves. Both these points are proved by Scripture and have been available to the eyes of faith ever since they were uttered. The point about the Gentiles is proved in Hosea, chapters one and two, and the point about the faithful remnant in Isaiah, chapters ten and eleven, and also in Isaiah 1.9. What distinguishes those who receive mercy from those who do not is faith in the crucified Messiah. This was prophesied in Isaiah 8.14; 28.16."

Before going on to consider how far the author of the Pastorals has reproduced Paul's line of thought, we should notice that Paul ends his chapter with a composite quotation, made up of Isaiah 8.14 and 28.16. The last line comes from Isaiah 28.16: "And he who believes in him will not be put to shame." The first part of Isaiah 28.16 runs: "Behold, I am laying in Zion for a foundation, a

stone, a tested stone, a precious cornerstone, of a sure foundation."
Then follows the line quoted by Paul. It is interesting to observe
that the author of the Pastorals has apparently taken the image of
a foundation with an inscription on it, or consisting of an inscription, from this passage. Thus Paul's "stone" quotation leads on to
the thought of 2 Timothy 2.19. But Isaiah 28.16 is also clearly in
the background of Ephesians 2.20 which offers an interesting
parallel to the Pastorals passage under consideration, and to
which we must return presently. Though there is much un-
certainty at present as to how far the *testimonia* system was used
by early Christian writers, it is hard to resist the conclusion that
Paul was using a catena of Old Testament quotations in Romans 9.
We meet the same accumulation of "stone" citations in 1 Peter
2.4–8. We might also compare Matthew 16.18. Our discussion of
1 Timothy 3.15 has already shown how far-reaching is this
language of stones and building in the New Testament.

Assuming then, as we must, that the author of the Pastorals was
consciously modelling himself on Romans 9.14–33, how far has
he reproduced Paul's thought? We might paraphrase his thought
thus: "There are some Christians, perhaps even Christian clergy,
who have proved themselves apostates. But the faithful remnant
stands firm by virtue of baptism, by calling, and by Christian
behaviour. We must not be surprised that inside the Church itself
some should prove to be reprobate. The important thing is that
you should free yourself from any association with such people
and thus become a useful servant." We have had to anticipate the
argument slightly with the reference to baptism, but this will be
explained later. The author of the Pastorals has realized that
Paul in Romans 9 is trying to explain why some are rejected and
some are elected, but he does not have Paul's sense of predestination.[3] He substitutes for the Jewish-Gentile contrast in Paul the
contrast in his own day between heretics or apostates and the
orthodox. In some ways his adaptation of the passage is appropriate enough, for he, like Paul, is trying to explain why some of
those who belong to the chosen race have been rejected and some
elected. But in his day the chosen race is the *tertium genus*, the

Christian Church, probably by this time consisting of a great majority of Gentiles, and he is trying to explain how it is that some from the very bosom of the Church have become apostate. It is essentially the same problem as is faced by the author of the First Epistle of St John (see 1 John 2.18–19). The solution offered by the author of the Pastorals appears to be an uneasy combination of both the answers to this problem given in the New Testament. The first quotation in 2 Timothy 2.19 leans towards John's answer: "The Lord knows who are his own", so not everyone apparently in the Church really belongs to it. The second quotation, and verses 21–2, suggest Paul's solution: the Church is a mixed body and contains those who may ultimately leave it. This is as clear an indication as we can demand that the author of the Pastorals is not one of the creative theologians of the New Testament.

We have said that this passage resembles Ephesians 2.20 in the sense that there also there is a "foundation", *themelios*. In Ephesians the foundation is "the apostles and prophets" with Christ as "the cornerstone". This in its turn reminds us of 1 Timothy 3.15, where we concluded that primarily Christ, and derivatively the Church, is the foundation. At the same time the word "seal", *sphragis*, points very definitely towards baptism. In Ephesians 1.13 and 4.30 the verb *sphragizō* is used of Christians having received the Spirit, very probably with reference to baptism.[4] In Ephesians 2.20 the apostles and prophets are the foundation and Christ the cornerstone, but, as an examination of the scholarly discussion which has taken place concerning this particular figure shows, it is by no means certain that the cornerstone is not part of the foundation, and it can be maintained that the apostles and prophets point back to the Old Testament period as well as referring to the new dispensation.

Some editors maintain that in Ephesians 2.20 the *akrogōniaios* is a foundation stone, for example von Soden who writes: "The leading thought is of the firm foundation, which in oriental building technique was composed by the corner stone." Jeremias admits that *akrogōniaios* as the LXX translation of *pinnath* in

Isaiah 28.16 did refer to the foundation stone, but he claims that this is a unique meaning for *akrogōniaios*. Everywhere else it means the "finishing stone", the last stone to be placed which completes the building, or at least a stone high up in the building and not in the foundation. He is sure that this is what it means in Ephesians 2.20 and thinks that the phrase is influenced by κεφαλὴ γωνίας "the headstone of the corner" from Psalm 118.22 (the two quotations occur together in 1 Peter 2.6–7).[5] M. Dibelius regards the case as proved (*An die Epheser* in loc. Eph. 2.20). The Hebrew word *pinnāh* has a number of meanings, all of which fall into one of two general senses, either "top" or "corner". For "top" we may quote Judges 20.2, where the word refers to the leaders or chiefs of the people, and the LXX (in the Codex Alexandrinus) translates by the vague word *klima* "top". For the "corner" sense we can point to Nehemiah 3.24,31, where it means apparently an angle in a wall, and the LXX translates fairly accurately with *kampē*. An interesting passage is Job 38.6, where *pinnāh* occurs in parallel with a word for "foundation", and the LXX translates λίθον γωνιαῖον. A similar passage occurs in Jeremiah 51.26, where the LXX translates with *gōnian*, and the parallel word with *themelion*. The impression one gains is that the word *akrogōniaios* does not have as exclusive a reference to the topmost stone as its etymology might suggest, and that to a Christian well versed in messianic texts *gōnia* would easily suggest *themelios* and vice versa. This impression is reinforced by R. J. McKelvey's illuminating discussion of the meaning of *akrogōniaios* in *New Testament Studies*.[6] He shows good reason for connecting it with the *Grundstein* or foundation stone in the temple, which, the rabbis believed, acted as a tap or plug against the waters under the earth. His conclusion is as follows: "We conclude then that the interpretation which explains *akrogōniaios* of Ephesians 2.20 as a top stone is to be abandoned in favour of the traditional understanding of *akrogōniaios* as a stone connected to the foundation of the building, which was located at one of the corners (probably the determinative corner) and bound together the walls and the foundation." This conclusion will bring the *themelios* of

2 Timothy 2.19 into even closer connection with the *akrogōniaios* of Ephesians 2.20 and the *hedraiōma* of 1 Timothy 3.15. In the Ephesians passage the connection between Christ and the faithful is explicit; in the two passages from the Pastorals it is implicit but can hardly be denied.

Kelly describes the foundation in 2 Timothy 2.19 as "the unshakeable core of genuine Christians at Ephesus",[7] and so also J. H. Bernard,[8] E. F. Brown,[9] A. R. C. Leaney, and E. F. Scott.[10] B. S. Easton thinks it refers to the Church, since the author goes on to speak of the household. He could hardly, however, have the whole Church in mind, since it seems very likely indeed that Hymenaeus and Philetus were baptized Christians. Both Spicq and Leaney suggest that *sphragis* refers to baptism. The word *stereos* "firm" in 2.19 may be an echo of Isaiah 8.14, because the word "stone" there in the phrase "stone of offence" is translated by Aquila (though not by the LXX) as *sterea petra* "hard rock". It is possible, therefore, that the author of the Pastorals had in mind the "hard rock" consisting of Christ when he wrote of the "hard foundation". It was after all, as we have seen, this very verse from Isaiah with which Paul rounds off the passage in Romans 9 that lies behind this one. At any rate, in view of the Old Testament and early Christian background against which 2 Timothy 2.19 is written, it is impossible not to believe that verse 19 refers to Christ as well as to the Church. We must be prepared to identify the "Lord" referred to twice in that verse with Christ.

It is, therefore, necessary to make a distinction between verse 19 and the rest of the passage we are examining. Verses 20–1 are the author's own adaptation of Romans 9.14–33 to the circumstances of the churches with which he was concerned. Verse 19 was probably inserted here by him in order to introduce this adaptation, and was therefore probably taken from some source. D-C suggests that the second quotation at least comes from an early Christian hymn, whose phraseology is influenced by the LXX. The most likely suggestion is that verse 19 originally stood in a baptismal context; we have the reference to the Church and to the *sphragis*, which probably indicates baptism. The two quotations, viewed simply as doctrine, would fit the theology of adult baptism very well. The first, "The Lord knows those who are his", reminds us of the divine initiative and calling; and the second, "Let every one who names the name of the Lord depart from iniquity", could well refer to the promises in baptism and the confession of the name of Jesus. Compare 1 Timothy 6.12–13.[11] If we can take it in this way, of course, there can be no doubt at all that Christ is referred to here. It may even be that this quotation was suggested to the author by Paul's stone-quotation at the end of Romans 9. And in any case, the verse is quite relevant to Romans 9, for both passages refer to the faithful remnant. Naturally, verses 19–20 in 2 Timothy 2 are not exactly similar to Romans 9, for Paul was thinking of the Christian Church as a whole as the faithful remnant, whereas the author of the Pastorals uses his passage to encourage the orthodox remnant within the Church to stand firm against the heretical teachers who have come out of the Church. But this adaptation is well within the scope of the author of the Pastorals, indeed it is what he does with considerable skill throughout his work.

Assuming then that we have in this passage a baptismal extract used to introduce a re-treatment of Romans 9.14–33, we must now examine the actual quotations in verses 19 rather more closely. We begin with the first: "The Lord knows those who are his". This is a loose quotation of Numbers 16.5, in the LXX, which we may render thus: "God has visited and knows those who are his and his holy ones." It occurs in the story of the revolt of Korah, Dathan, and Abiram against the authority of Moses and Aaron. This sentence is Moses' first reply to the rebels. It is significant that in the Pastorals "the Lord" has been substituted for "God" and indicates that Christ is thought of here as the Lord. The incident related in Numbers would, as a matter of fact, be very appropriate to the author's situation. He too is facing the rejection of his authority by members of his own group. Perhaps this is why he chose this particular quotation. It is interesting to observe that there is in the story of the revolt against Moses an anticipation of the theme of the next quotation also, for in

Numbers 16.21 God says to Moses: "Separate yourselves from among this congregation that I may consume them in a moment", and in verse 27 we read: "So they got away [LXX ἀπέστησαν, same word as in 2 Timothy 2.19] from about the dwelling of Korah, Dathan, and Abiram." It may be worth noting that Moses and Aaron constantly name the name of the Lord in the course of the narrative, and actually call upon him in verse 22: "O God, the God of the spirits of all flesh." The rebels for their part do not call on the name at all, though they do use the divine Name twice during their only speech in verse 3. But it is not necessary to assume that the author of the Pastorals or his source intended this significance.

At any rate the first quotation, whose source is undoubted, leads on to the second one, whose source is not. In fact there is no exact parallel for this in all Old Testament literature, and D-C, as we have seen, is driven to the conclusion that the author is not quoting Scripture at all, but merely citing a Christian hymn influenced by LXX phraseology. The nearest parallel is probably Isaiah 52.11:

> Depart, depart, go out thence,
>   touch no unclean thing;
> go out from the midst of her, purify yourselves,
>   you who bear the vessels of the Lord.

The only link is really "Depart", which is ἀπόστητε in the LXX, as in 2 Timothy 2.19. There is a teasing echo of all this in Romans 15.20:

> Thus making it my ambition to preach the gospel not where Christ has already been named, lest I build on another man's foundation, but as it is written:
>   "They shall see who have never been told of him,
>   and they shall understand who have never heard of him."

This quotation comes from Isaiah 52.15, only four verses beyond the passage just referred to. It is tempting to see some significance in this triple concurrence: naming the name of Christ, building on a foundation, quoting from an evangelical passage in Isaiah.

But Paul's foundation is not quite that of 2 Timothy 2.19 (though in 1 Corinthians 3.11 Paul identifies the two), and Isaiah 52.11 has only a tenuous connection with 2 Timothy 2.19.[12] The utmost one could suggest is that Paul and another early Christian theologian have treated the same passage in Isaiah, one with evangelism, and one with baptism in view, both concerned for building up the Church.

The other part of the second quotation, "every one who names the name of the Lord", has plenty of Old Testament background. The exact Greek phrase occurs in the LXX translation of Leviticus 24.16: "He who names the name of the Lord shall surely die". The LXX translation is a literal rendering of the Hebrew, which the RSV translates: "He who blasphemes the name of the Lord shall be put to death." The Hebrew verb *nāqabh* means literally "to prick" hence "designate", so the LXX has got the literal sense, but it is plain from the context that the RSV translators are right in taking the meaning as "blaspheme". It occurs in the incident of the half-breed who quarrelled with an Israelite and, in the course of the quarrel, "blasphemed the Name, and cursed". It is likely that he is represented as having pronounced the divine Name in order to bring down a curse on his enemy. By the time that this passage was written, it may well be that the reluctance to pronounce the divine Name which was so marked in later Judaism was already apparent.[10] Compare Ben Sira 23.10b:

> So also the man who always swears and utters the Name
> will not be cleansed from sin.

Certainly the translators of the LXX would have considered the uttering of the Name in such a context as an undoubted example of blasphemy, and this is made plain by their simple equation of naming the name with an act of blasphemy worthy of death. Many instances of prohibition to mention the names of other gods occur in the Old Testament (e.g. Exod. 23.13; Josh. 23.7). This was no doubt because to mention the name was to implicate oneself to some extent with the one named. H. Bietenhard has suggested that there is no exact Hebrew equivalent to ὀνομάζειν τὸ ὄνομα because there is in Hebrew no verb from *shem* "name" to correspond to the Greek ὀνομάζειν.[14] But it seems more likely that the Hebrews did not write "naming the name" in so many words because they could write the divine Name without any scruple, as could not be done in Greek, and that therefore they did not have great need of a written periphrasis as Greek did.

In the Mishnah uttering the divine Name is treated as blasphemy: "The blasphemer is punished only if he utters the divine Name."[15] Great precautions were to be taken to ensure that the Name was not unnecessarily uttered during a trial for blasphemy. Only one of the witnesses who heard it uttered is required to repeat it in the presence of the judges, and only then in conditions of the greatest secrecy. The Talmud then goes on to discuss whether *nāqabh* really means "to curse". Leviticus 24.11 is cited: "And the Israelite woman's son blasphemed the Name and cursed." One opinion is put forward to the effect that this verse proves that uttering the Name and cursing were identical, since the Hebrew uses two verbs *wayyiqqōbh* (literally "uttered") and *wayᵃqallel* ("cursed"). In fact one suspects that the man used the divine Name in order to invoke a curse on someone else, but the passage does show that among the rabbis uttering the divine Name was in itself blasphemy, except in the most carefully defined circumstances.

The Targum on Leviticus 24.10-23 adds some midrashic details about the blasphemer.[16] He was a son of the Egyptian who had killed the Israelite in Egypt (presumably a reference to Exod. 2.11). He tried to pitch his tent with the tribe of Dan, but they would not permit him. This was the cause of the quarrel. When his case was tried and he had lost it, he came out from the house of judgement and "he expressed and uttered the great and glorious Name of Manifestation which he had heard at Sinai, and defied and execrated". Leviticus 24.15-16 is paraphrased thus: "Whosoever expresseth and revileth the Name of the Lord shall be put to death". Thus, though the Targum heaps other sins on the blasphemer as well, the pronunciation of the Tetragrammaton is certainly the first charge on the sheet.

Confirmation for the interpretation advanced here of the words "Let every one who names the name of the Lord depart from iniquity" can be found in a passage of the *Manual of Discipline* of the Dead Sea Scrolls. P. Wernberg-Møller translates vi. 27— vii.1 as follows:

> [The one w]ho makes an oath in the honoured name . . . If anybody curses (God), either because of being terror-struck with affliction, or because of any other reason he may have, while reciting from the Book or saying benedictions—he (or they) shall exclude him.[17]

The Hebrew is literally "he who makes mention of a thing (or a word) in the honoured Name",[18] but Wernberg-Møller refers to Isaiah 48.1 as evidence that the meaning is "to take an oath in the name". In Isaiah 48.1 "to swear in the name of the Lord" is parallel to "to make mention of the God of Israel". Millar Burrows translates: "Any man who mentions anything by the Name which is honoured above all . . ."[19] T. H. Gaster, still more clearly, renders it: "If a man, in speaking about anything, mention that name which is honoured above all . . ."[20] It is thus fairly certain that there is a prohibition against mentioning the divine Name under any circumstances. The reference to the possibility of cursing God while reading from the book or uttering benedictions is most interesting. The word for "curse God" is QLL, without any object expressed, but the parallel in Leviticus 24.11 makes it plain that this means "to blaspheme by mentioning the divine Name"; "and the Israelite woman's son blasphemed the Name, and cursed", where "and cursed" is *way^aqallel*. I suggest that the situation envisaged in Manual of Discipline vii. 1 is one in which, through distraction caused by personal affliction or some other reason, the reader pronounces the divine Name instead of substituting *Adonai*. T. H. Gaster translates "in a moment of stress, or for some other personal reason".[21] Thus in the Qumran documents we find just the same stringent prohibition against naming the name. The contrast with the Christian dispensation is clear indeed. In Qumran even inadvertent pronunciation of the name is punished. In Christianity all believers are privileged to pronounce it openly, though such a privilege carries with it obligations for conduct.

In view of the significance of "naming the Name" in the LXX and in subsequent literature, the quotation in 2 Timothy 2.19 takes on great significance. The Name has now been disclosed. The Tetragrammaton is now recognized as indicating 'Ιησοῦς and Christians are free to name the name with that boldness of which both Paul and the author of the Epistle to the Hebrews speak. What was blasphemy under the Law is the prerogative of every true Israelite under grace. Thus, this passage provides a valuable link with all those other places in the New Testament where the privilege of Christians is emphasized. Paul in 2 Corinthians 3 argues that now all Christians stand where formerly only Moses stood and can view the divine presence with unveiled face. The author of the Epistle to the Hebrews claims in Hebrews 10 that all Christians can now enter into the holy of holies through the veil. And our author himself, by his use of the Christian midrash in 1 Timothy 3.15, claims that all Christians can be present in the innermost sanctuary, where the Sh^ekīnāh of God is to be met with in the person of Christ. The second quotation in 2 Timothy 2.19 is therefore deeply christological in meaning, despite the fact that the name of Christ does not occur in it. Its relation to the first is perfectly clear if we see both quotations as originally occurring in a baptismal context: it defines the responsibilities ("depart from iniquity") and privileges ("naming the name of the Lord") of Christians conferred in baptism, just as the first quotation implies the promise and election of God. Daniélou regards "the Name" as one of the theological categories to describe the Word which Jewish Christianity used (see La Théologie du Judéo-Christianisme, pp. 200 ff). One can hardly describe the usage in 2 Timothy 2.19 as directly influenced by Jewish Christianity, but the source from which the author of the Pastorals took this sentence may well have been so influenced. One might even account for the difficulty in finding an exact scriptural source for the second quotation by saying that it is an example of a Jewish-Christian targum, as expounded by K. Stendahl and Daniélou.

If we stand back for a moment and view the whole passage of 2 Timothy 2.19–21 in perspective, we may describe it as an excellent example of the technique of the author of the Pastorals. He wanted a passage which would confirm his claim to be writing in Paul's tradition, refute the claim of the dissident teachers to be the true Church, and reassure the faithful in his area. He undertakes a retreatment of a difficult passage in Romans, a perfectly legitimate activity from his point of view, since Paul was dealing with fundamentally the same problem as himself, the problem of apostasy. But he strengthens his own adaptation of Paul by means of a quotation from one of his sources. We must not rashly speculate about the nature of the source, but it is safe to assume that it was connected with baptism. This material is appropriate to his purpose in more than one way; it refers specifically to the Church as the true faithful remnant, it contains an echo of the story of the revolt against Moses in the wilderness, thereby suggesting that the dissidents in the author's day were on the wrong side, and it brings out a fundamental theological insight common to more than one tradition in the New Testament, the privilege of Christians as compared to Jews (we must not forget that the opposition which the author was facing had a strong Jewish element). All in all we may say that in this passage the author of the Pastorals is at one and the same time showing fairly clearly that he is not Paul and vindicating his own peculiar place in the development of the New Testament.

4

Inspired Scripture:
2 Timothy 3.14–17

But as for you, continue in what you have learned and have firmly believed, knowing from whom you learned it and how from childhood you have been acquainted with the sacred writings which are able to instruct you for salvation through faith in Christ Jesus. Every scripture inspired by God is also profitable[1] for teaching, for reproof, for correction, and for training in righteousness, that the man of God may be complete, equipped for every good work.

The translation "the sacred writings" represents a phrase in the Greek which has, according to the best MS. authority, no article. It is a most un-Pauline phrase. D-C has shown clearly that it comes from Philo. It is Philo's regular method of referring to the LXX. It can have no other meaning here: the author thinks of the Old Testament as he knew it as inspired scripture. Thus Brown's translation "religious education" and Lock's[2] "sacred letters" are equally wide of the mark, nor is there much evidence to support Scott's suggestion that the phrase is deliberately left vague in order to include the intertestamental literature and the earliest books of the New Testament.

The phrase translated "from childhood" might be better rendered "from babyhood". *Brephos* is always used in the New Testament of very small children. S-B brings plenty of evidence to show that the Hebrew child was first instructed in the scriptures at the age of five or six.[3] No doubt the phrase does refer to Jewish usage carried over into the life of the Christian Church. On the other hand, it is important to realize that it is a Christian who is writing, and, in the view of an early Christian, although what we call the Old Testament scriptures were able to instruct one for salvation, they will not necessarily do so unless interpreted by faith and with Christ as the clue. Thus C. K. Barrett rightly points out that "through faith in Christ Jesus" is no conventional phrase here. Indeed, if we press the point literally, Timothy probably was not instructed in Christianity in the scriptures from infancy, for we cannot be at all sure that his mother was a Christian, when he was born. It seems unlikely on the evidence. Thus, though the author is using rather un-Pauline language here, his thought is thoroughly in line with Paul's, as we shall be seeing when we come to examine the relevance of Romans 15.1–6 for this passage.

Next we must consider the phrase, "Every scripture inspired by God is also profitable for teaching". The Greek is πᾶσα γραφὴ θεόπνευστος καὶ ὠφέλιμος πρὸς διδασκαλίαν. In the New Testament γραφή in the singular can have only two meanings, either "a passage of scripture" or "the scriptures as a whole". When the New Testament writers wish to refer to the scriptures as a whole they normally use the plural αἱ γραφαί, but there are places where ἡ γραφή means "the Bible". For example, in John 10.35 "scripture cannot be broken" ἡ γραφή no doubt refers to the Old Testament as a whole; but it is doubtful if any other examples of this use can be found in any of the four Gospels. In Paul ἡ γραφή usually means one particular passage of scripture; but Paul can use ἡ γραφή for the sense of the Bible as a whole: a good example is Galatians 3.22: "But the scripture consigned all things to sin". G. Schrenk points out that in the parallel verse in Romans 11.32 Paul writes: "God has consigned all men to disobedience."[4] The two instances in the Petrine Epistles both fall into this category: 1 Peter 2.6, "it stands in scripture" means "it is written in the Bible". Likewise in 2 Peter 1.20, but we shall be discussing that passage presently. It is important to notice that the phrase in 2 Timothy 3.16 cannot possibly mean "a book of scripture". As Schrenk says: "γραφή for a single book of the Bible is completely absent from the New Testament, though it is a very frequent usage in Hellenistic Judaism."

We have said that the phrase in 2 Timothy 3.16 cannot possibly mean "every book of the Old Testament". But we can go further than this and assert that it cannot either mean "the whole Bible". To produce the meaning "the whole Bible" one would have to have πᾶσα ἡ γραφή. Thus πᾶσα γραφή can mean only one thing here, "every passage of scripture". This is not accepted by all editors: Guthrie,[5] for example, translates: "All Scripture is inspired by God . . .", and Spicq offers: "Toute écriture, inspirée de Dieu . . .". Easton also follows this rendering.[6] RSV surprisingly prefers this rendering also, having in the text: "All scripture is inspired . . ." This is why we have preferred to print the marginal rendering, though even this is not altogether satisfactory.

From this it follows that we must prefer the translation: "Every passage of scripture is inspired and is profitable. . . ". Admittedly there is nothing in either grammar or syntax to prevent us taking it as many editors do: "Every inspired passage of scripture is also profitable. . . ". This is preferred by Bernard, D-C, NEB, and Barrett. But considerations of sense must surely weigh against this. If the author wrote "Every inspired passage of scripture is profitable . . .", he was implying that there could be an uninspired passage of scripture, but this is precisely the view that he is opposing. He is claiming that every passage in scripture is inspired and may therefore also be used for various purposes, paedagogic, apologetic, and devotional. The translation we have preferred, "Every passage of scripture is inspired and is profitable . . .", is approved by Jeremias and Kelly. We must assume that some of the author's opponents were casting aspersions on some parts of the Old Testament. This can hardly be an incipient Marcionism, for Marcion rejected the entire Old Testament.

In what sense did the author think of the Old Testament as inspired? The word for "inspired", *theopneustos*, is unique in the

New Testament and LXX, and does not occur in Philo. It is found in roughly contemporary pagan writers, for example Plutarch uses it of dreams. It is difficult to imagine a Hebrew or Aramaic word of which it could be a translation. But we can say with confidence that though Philo does not use it, it exactly expresses Philo's idea of the relation of scripture to the authors of scripture. What *theopneustos* implies is that the author of scripture is possessed by God and therefore what he writes is inspired by God. For example, in *De Confusione Linguarum* 44 he quotes Jeremiah 15.10 and then describes the prophet as καταπνευσθεὶς ἐνθουσιῶν ἀπεφθέγξατο, "being inspired and divinely possessed he made this utterance". In *De Somniis* 1. 254, he says of Samuel: "not really on the human plane at all, but somehow possessed and mastered by the divine frenzy". This divine frenzy is frequently predicated of Moses, as for example in *De Vita Mosis* I. 175: "He became possessed by God, being inspired [καταπνευσθεὶς] by the spirit which usually visited him, he uttered oracles [θεσπίζει] and prophesied as follows", then comes Exodus 14.13. In *De Vita Mosis* II. 251. Philo writes of Moses "being no longer his own master, he is carried away by God and utters the following oracles". A very interesting passage occurs in *Questions on Exodus* I. 49. Philo discusses the suggestion that Moses declared the Law to Israel knowing that most of those who heard it would be destroyed because of the incident of the golden calf. But he dismisses this idea: "But he who says this should bear in mind that every prophetic soul is divinely inspired and prophesies many future things not so much by reflecting as through divine madness and certainty."[7] Thus Philo is repudiating the idea that the authors of scripture necessarily had any notion of what they were saying. They did not reflect and then write down; they wrote as men inspired. They were not so much prophets as mediums. This can apply even to men whose character Philo condemns. Thus in *De Vita Mosis* I. 266–77, where he is discussing the story of Balaam in Numbers 22—4, though he describes in sombre colours Balaam's shocking character and calls him a magician (*magos*), he fully admits Balaam's divine inspiration when he utters his oracles. This inspiration extends of course to the text of scripture, otherwise it would be ineffective. Thus Philo frequently refers to the scriptures as *chrēsmoi*, "oracles" (for example, *De Cherubim* 124; *Quod Deterior Potiori Insidiari Solet* 74).

Various scholars have suggested that there is some sort of contrast to be found between Paul's attitude to the Old Testament and that of other later New Testament authors. Easton, for example, emphasizes the contrast between Paul and the author of the Pastorals: "While Paul was an adept at discovering 'spiritual' meanings in unlikely texts (1 Cor. 9.9; 10.11; etc.), he emphatically did not regard the Old Testament as the Christians' moral guide; his ethic was based on Jesus' law of love . . . The Pastor is perfectly illustrated by Clement's constant appeal to the Old Testament for moral instruction." This is true, but hardly to the point. The question is not: From what source did Paul take his moral instruction? But: In what sense did Paul regard the Old Testament as inspired? We must not forget that Paul says explicitly in Romans 15.4 that "whatever was written in former days was written for our instruction". Schrenk suggests that in primitive Christianity the personality of the various writers of the Old Testament was more emphasized than in Judaism, but that this does not alter the fact that God was thought of as speaking through all of them. Jeremias, however, goes much farther than this. In his commentary on this passage he claims that Palestinian Judaism allowed a place for the human writers, but the Diaspora, as represented by Philo, inclined to a doctrine of inspiration in which the writers were merely the tools of the Spirit. Jesus and Paul, he says, preferred the Palestinian tradition, but Hebrews is more Philonic.[8]

This is not the place to discuss Paul's view of the inspiration of scripture, though it does not seem that Jeremias has done full justice to those passages in which Paul understands the pre-existent Christ to be speaking through the mouth of Psalmist, prophet, or even through Moses. The question is rather: On which side must we rank this passage in 2 Timothy 3.16? In order to decide this question, we must first consider three other passages in the New Testament, 1 Peter 1.10–12; 2 Peter 1.19–21; 2.15–16. The 1 Peter passage runs:

> The prophets who prophesied of the grace that was to be yours searched and inquired about this salvation; they inquired what person or time was indicated by the Spirit of Christ within them when predicting the sufferings of Christ and the subsequent glory. It was revealed to them that they were serving not themselves but you, in the things which have just been announced to you by those who preached the good news to you through the Holy Spirit sent from heaven.

In my book *Jesus Christ in the Old Testament* (pp. 133 ff), I argued that this passage is in fact a midrash on Habakkuk 2.1–4. In the Habakkuk passage the prophet could well be imagined to be searching and seeking as to when the end time would be during which the events he foretold should come to pass. The prophet is represented as standing on his watch to see what the Lord would reveal; and the LXX, slightly mistranslating the Hebrew, has "to see what he will speak in me". This seems to correspond fairly closely with what we find in these verses in 1 Peter. At any rate few people today would be found to agree with E. G. Selwyn's contention that Christian prophets are meant.[9]

There is also a passage in the Qumran Commentary on Habakkuk which throws a very interesting light on 1 Peter 1.10–12. The author of the Commentary writes as follows about Habakkuk 2.1–2:[10] "And God told Habakkuk to write the things that were to come upon the last generation, but the consummation of the period he did not make known to him. And as for what it says, *that he may run who reads it*, this means the teacher of righteousness, to whom God made known all the mysteries of the words of his servants the prophets." F. F. Bruce says that, according to the scheme of the Qumran sectaries, the *rāz*, or "mystery", was made known to the prophets, but the *pesher*, its "interpretation", was communicated only to the Teacher of Righteousness.[11] Here then we have a concept very similar to that in 1 Peter: in both the documents God entrusts his secrets to the prophets, but they do not themselves know when or how these secrets (concerning the end-time) will be fulfilled. There are, of course, significant differences also: Christians do not need a Teacher of Righteousness to give them the *pesher*, because the prophecies have already been fulfilled in Jesus. Also, whereas among the Qumran sectaries it was the faithful who "searched and inquired" in the Law, the Christian writer thinks of the prophets themselves as doing this. Behind the ἐξεζήτησαν καὶ ἐξηραύνησαν of 1 Peter we can surely detect the verb *dārash* which played such an important part in the Qumran sect. In fact ἐκζητεῖν is a frequent translation for *dārash* in the LXX.

It is even possible that we can trace a further parallel with Qumran. Otto Betz points out that in the Manual of Discipline viii.16. the prophets are described as revealing God's will through the Holy Spirit: "to do according to all that has been revealed from time to time, and as the prophets revealed by his (*sc.* God's) Holy Spirit".[12] Betz also claims that in the Damascus Document ii.12 the prophets are described as "anointed by the Spirit". This passage, is, however, very obscure. It is not clear whether the prophets are being alluded to or the interpreters in the Qumran sect; some scholars translate the phrase differently. For example, Millar Burrows offers: "And he caused them to know by his anointed his Holy Spirit."[13] But in any case it is clear that according to the Qumran sectaries the Old Testament prophets spoke by the Holy Spirit. Once again we cannot fail to note the specifically Christian *differentia* in 1 Peter at the same time as we note the resemblance to Qumran: the prophets were inspired by "the Spirit of Christ", who is implicitly identified with the Holy Spirit. Thus the 1 Peter passage does seem to have a Palestinian background: its doctrine of inspiration has much in common with the Qumran sectaries.

T. W. Manson, in reviewing Selwyn's commentary when it first appeared,[14] suggested that the "angels" mentioned at the end of verse 12 represent the same word in Aramaic as is represented by "kings" in Luke 10.23 and "righteous men" in Matthew 13.17, and that the passage in 1 Peter is a midrash on the original saying, perhaps written by one who originally heard it uttered by Jesus. But surely the whole point of the saying is the distinction between the prophets, who are deeply concerned with the Christian dispensation, and the angels, who are not integrally connected with it. The author represents the prophets as now in his day enjoying the fruits of the prophecies which they had previously made; cf. Hebrews 11.39 "that apart from us they should not be made perfect". The prophets share in the consummation as the angels do not.

We now turn to 2 Peter 1.20–1:

> First of all you must understand this, that no prophecy of scripture is a matter of one's own interpretation, because no prophecy ever came by the impulse of man, but men moved by the Holy Spirit spoke from God.[15]

The Greek for "no prophecy of scripture" is of private interpretation is πᾶσα προφητεία γραφῆς ἰδίας ἐπιλύσεως οὐ γίνεται. We should note here that *graphē* must have the sense of "the scriptures as a whole". C. Bigg is no doubt right in insisting that the author is thinking solely of the Hebrew prophets.[16] The phrase should be taken in its context. In the previous verse we read: "We have this prophetic verse made sure", and this follows the well-known reference to the Transfiguration. H. von Soden says that the "private interpretation" (ἰδίας ἐπιλύσεως) is contrasted with the "voice borne . . . by the Majestic Glory" of verse 17.[17] This is true as far as it goes, but there is more to it than that: the author is probably wishing to imply that the voice of the prophets in Old Testament scripture is as infallible as the voice from heaven heard at the transfiguration; and no doubt Cranfield is right in adding: "The fact that the Old Testament promises have already been to so large an extent fulfilled (in Christ) is the guarantee that that which is still unfulfilled— the promise of the final glorious manifestation of God's kingdom will not fail of fulfilment."[18]

What strikes one most forcibly about this passage is how faithful it is to Philo's conception of inspiration. Pseudo-Peter says that prophecy was not given by men's will, and Philo suggests that Samuel was no longer on the human plane when he spoke his utterances. Pseudo-Peter speaks of men being carried away (φερόμενοι) by the Holy Spirit; Philo speaks of Moses being "carried away by God (θεοφορεῖται) in *De Vita Mosis* II. 251. The author of 2 Peter has really got two points here which he wishes to emphasize: (*a*) the prophets did not just utter their own thoughts, however in accordance with God's will they might have been; they uttered God's words when he chose to inspire them[19] (compare Philo, *Questions on Exodus* I. 49, quoted above), (*b*) their prophecies are not capable of being interpreted by anyone or by any means; they can only be understood, as Cranfield says, "with the help of the Holy Spirit, and in the fellowship of the faithful"; in other words, the opposite of "private interpretation" is christological interpretation. But this means that this passage in 2 Peter is exactly in line with 2 Timothy 3.15–16, from which we began. In the Pastorals passage the divine inspiration of the Old Testament scriptures is emphasized, and it is said explicitly that faith in Jesus Christ is needed in order to benefit from them. Exactly the same message is contained here, though expressed in very different words.

The third passage is 2 Peter 2.15–16:

> Forsaking the right way they have gone astray; they have followed the way of Balaam, the son of Beor, who loved gain from wrongdoing, but was rebuked for his own transgression; a dumb ass spoke with human voice and restrained the prophet's madness.

We have noted that Philo has no hesitation in regarding Balaam as an inspired prophet despite his deplorable moral character. Balaam might therefore seem to be the acid test for the Philonic theory of inspiration. But in fact one could imagine a little more searching test, one would call it a *reductio ad absurdum* if one had any reason to think that the author of 2 Peter had any sense of humour. It is Balaam's ass. If a writer can regard the ass as uttering an inspired statement, then he is indeed a committed member of Philo's school of inspiration. Philo himself does not challenge this ultimate test; though he deals with the story of Balaam as we have seen, he makes no mention of the incident of the speaking ass. We may reasonably conjecture that he found it embarrassing and preferred not to undertake the task of defending it or (more likely) allegorizing it. The author of 2 Peter, however, submits to the test and emerges unscathed; he has no doubt whatever about the divine inspiration of either Balaam or his ass.

The passage which he has in mind is Numbers 22.28: "Then the Lord opened the mouth of the ass, and she said to Balaam . . .". The fact that he uses the emphatic word φθεγξάμενον shows that he regards the ass's utterance as an inspired one. It is a word frequently used by Philo for inspired utterances (cf. *De Confusione Linguarum* 44, ἀνεφθέγξατο). Again, despite his emphatic condemnation of Balaam, he describes him as "the prophet". Here then we find the author of 2 Peter applying Philo's theory of inspiration without scruple to the incident of Balaam's ass; both ass and reprobate prophet are the instruments of the Holy Spirit.

Though Philo disregards the incident, Josephus does not. In *Antiquities* IV. 6.3, he gives a perfectly straightforward account of the ass rebuking Balaam. He rather emphasizes that the ass spoke with a human voice, and that this was by God's special providence. His words are: "By the will of God the ass received a human voice and rebuked Balaam . . . Balaam was alarmed by the human voice of the she-ass."[20] The author of 2 Peter also emphasizes the human voice of the ass; it may even be that he was influenced by reading Josephus' account.

The Rabbis, of course, have no doubts at all about the divinely inspired nature of the ass's utterance. One account says it was the *Memra'* of Adonai that opened the ass's mouth.[21] They are even more condemnatory of Balaam than either Philo or the author of 2 Peter, for they accuse him of having immoral relations with the she-ass. They do, however, show a certain amount of perplexity about his plenary inspiration: "Seeing that he did not know the mind of his ass," they ask, "could he know the mind of the Most High?" (as he claims to do in Numbers 24.4,16). They answer that in fact he did know how to gauge the exact moment when the most High was angry (this is on the basis of Micah 6.5).[22]

When we look at these four passages together, 2 Timothy 3.14–17; 1 Peter 1.10–12; 2 Peter 1.19–21; 2.15–16, surely we cannot fail to see that they belong together. They are all interested in the inspiration of scripture, and they all take a largely automatic or Philonic view of the nature of that inspiration. Among the four, it is true, the 1 Peter passage stands apart from the rest. It witnesses to the sort of doctrine of scriptural inspiration which is found also in Qumran. This is like Philo's in that the scriptural writers are thought of as mere instruments of the divine afflatus, but unlike Philo in that it is strongly eschatological. It is only the end-time that reveals the true fulfilment of the prophetic utterances. However, the author of 1 Peter represents the prophets as taking a keen interest in the meaning of their inspired utterances, and this is a feature of which there is as yet no trace in the Qumran documents. What 1 Peter has in common with the other three passages (that in the Pastorals and those in 2 Peter) is an interest in the mode of inspiration. These last three obviously stand together; they belong to the world of Christianity strongly influenced by Hellenistic Judaism.

But there is one other passage in the New Testament with which we must compare 2 Timothy 3.14–17, and that is Romans 15.1–6. We may quote verses 4–6:

> For whatever was written in former days was written for our instruction, that by steadfastness and by the encouragement of the scriptures we might have hope. May the God of steadfastness and encouragement grant you to live in such harmony with one another, in accord with Christ Jesus, that together you may with one voice glorify the God and Father of our Lord Jesus Christ.

Editors have, of course, noticed the general similarity which this passage bears to 2 Timothy 3.14–17; but it may be worth considering whether in fact the 2 Timothy passage may not be deliberately modelled on the passage in Romans 15. We might draw out the points of resemblance thus:

ROMANS 15.4–6	2 TIMOTHY 3.16–17
whatever was written in former days	every scripture inspired by God
instruction	teaching[23]
steadfastness	training
encouragement	correction
you	the man of God

There is, of course, only a very general parallelism here, but we can explain the modifications which the author of the Pastorals has made. Both writers are saying essentially the same thing, that the Old Testament scriptures find their fulfilment in Jesus Christ and therefore, as understood by Christians, can give knowledge about Christ and can aid the Christian in living the Christian life. The author of the Pastorals has expressed these uses of scripture in words different from Paul's, though corresponding to them. Both agree that the scriptures can teach us about Christ. Where Paul says that we can receive encouragement (that great word of his, *paraklēsis*), the author of the Pastorals says that we receive correction; where Paul says that they can help us to be steadfast, the author says that they help for training in Christianity. These last two words in the Pastorals reflect accurately his tendency to draw on pagan sources for his moral teaching, as the phrase παιδεία καὶ ἐπανόρθωσις is used by Epictetus to describe the aim of the mysteries.[24] Paul speaks of these fruits of the scriptures as being available for all Christians: "grant you to live in such harmony". The author of the Pastorals is thinking primarily of their advantage to the ordained minister: "that the man of God may be complete". It is a distinctive feature of the Pastorals that what is applied by Paul to the whole local congregation is applied by the author of the Pastorals to the local minister; compare 2 Timothy 1.8 with Philippians 1.29–30. It is true that the author of the Pastorals adds one more use to which the scriptures can be put, "reproof". This seems to mean the refutation of heretics. Paradoxically enough, however, it is Paul who gives us the example of refuting false teachers by means of scripture. The author of the Pastorals does not use scripture for this purpose, but normally uses straightforward condemnation and abuse instead. In fact, one could say that a comparison of 2 Timothy 3.14–17 with Romans 15.1–6 neatly illustrates the relationship which exists between the Pastoral Epistles and the genuinely Pauline writings.

One question, however, remains to be answered: Is there in fact any difference between Paul and the authors of the Pastorals and of the Petrine Epistles, as far as their attitude to the inspiration of the scriptures is concerned? They express their ideas, it is true, in different language; indeed, in this respect we should have to envisage three ways of saying it, that of Paul, that of the author of 1 Peter, and that common to the Pastorals and 2 Peter. But is there any real difference of approach to the doctrine of the inspiration of the scriptures? I think we can say that there is, and that it consists in this: Paul was not interested in the actual mode of inspiration, while all the others were. In this context, it is very instructive to refer to Dom Jacques Dupont's discussion of inspiration in his great study *Gnosis*.[25] He shows that Paul certainly thought of *pneuma* as incompatible with *nous* in the case of those who spoke with tongues. But nowhere does Paul suggest that the writers of the Old Testament scriptures were in the same position as those who uttered glossolalia. This, surely, is where the difference from Philo is clearest. For Philo the prophets of old were exactly in this position. Here then is where a clear line can be drawn between Paul on the one hand and on the other the authors of the Pastorals and 2 Peter. The First Epistle of Peter is, as we have seen, in yet a different category. It is significant that the passages in the Pastorals and in the Petrines all emphasize the fact of divine inspiration. Paul does not. It is not that Paul thought the scriptures were not inspired; quite the contrary, they are just as authoritative for him as for the others. It is rather that he seems to treat them more directly as the utterances of God or Christ, without stopping to consider the mode of inspiration. Just before the verses we have quoted from Romans 15, Paul has cited a line from the Psalms, and he does so in order to illustrate a characteristic of Christ, his self-giving love. It seems plain from the context that he understands Christ as having personally uttered the words: "The reproaches of those who reproached thee fell on me". He uttered them, of course, through the mouth of David, but they can be received as Christ's utterance and therefore as affording information about Christ. It is perhaps true to say therefore that in his approach to inspiration Paul has his own unique doctrine. He believed as fervently as they did in the inspiration of the scriptures, but he shows no traces of a doctrine of "possession" as they undoubtedly do.

5

The Mediator:
1 Timothy 2.5–6

For there is one God, and there is one mediator between God and men, the man Christ Jesus, who gave himself as a ransom for all, the testimony to which was borne at the proper time.

Naturally these verses have been claimed by many modern editors as constituting some sort of a formula, whether liturgical, credal, or catechetical (it is very precarious to attempt to distinguish among these categories in the New Testament). Thus B. S. Easton calls them liturgical, "a Christian version of the Jewish Sh*e*ma*c*". A. J. B. Higgins describes them as part of "a primitive creed."[1] D-C agrees that they are liturgical, and J. N. D. Kelly accepts them as a catechetical or liturgical formula. P. Carrington goes so far as to suggest that they are "a piece of a eucharistic anaphora".[2] We are not concerned here with the relation of verse 6 to Mark 10.45 except in so far as it can throw light on the provenance of the passage as a whole. It is in the word "mediator" that we are particularly interested.

The Greek word *mesitēs* is used by Paul of Moses in Galatians 3.19–20, where the fact that the old covenant required the services of a human mediator is treated as a sign of its inferiority.[3] It is also used three times in Hebrews of Christ as the mediator of a new covenant (8.6; 9.15; 12.24; cf. also 6.17 for the verb). Philo uses the word of Moses and indeed in Judaism Moses is the mediator *par excellence*; but Philo can also use it of angels and of the Logos. Oepke[4] suggests that here, because of the use of the word *mesitēs*, Christ is thought of as the antitype of Moses.

Much, however, depends on whether Paul is taken as the author of this passage. It does not seem likely, it must be confessed, that he could easily use the word *mesitēs* of Christ, having used it of Moses in a context where the presence of a mediator implies inferiority. It does not therefore look as if we ought to seek the origin of the word in a context where the Law is in question. Daniélou, in *Théologie du Judéo-Christianisme* (p. 175), suggests that in this phrase we have an echo of Jewish-Christian theology, which sometimes identified Christ with Michael, and he quotes Testament of Dan VI. 2, where Michael is described as "a mediator between God and man". This view depends on the assumption that this passage in the Testament of Dan is of Jewish-Christian origin.[5] In any case it is not necessarily incompatible with the view that the formula in 1 Timothy 2.5 is influenced by the Book of Job, as we maintain below. Job, after all, has an absolutely explicit reference to angelic mediation in 33.23 (see note 8 on p. 127 below). One who was prepared to identify the Word with Michael would naturally be interested in Job 9.33.

I suggest, therefore, that the word originally came from the LXX of Job 9.33, the only occurrence of the word in the LXX.[6] When we look at it in its context in Job, we cannot fail to notice how relevant it would seem to an early Christian, particularly perhaps in a post-Pauline era. We may translate the LXX of Job 9.32–3 as follows:

> For thou art not a man like me [ἄνθρωπος κατ᾽ ἐμέ] to whom
>   I might reply,
> That we might come together to judgement.
> I wish there were our mediator and reprover [ὁ μεσίτης ἡμῶν καὶ
>   ἐλέγχων]
> And one to hear the case between us both.

In its septuagintal form this passage has two key words in common with 1 Timothy 2.5–6, μεσίτης and ἄνθρωπος. Job has complained that God is not a man, and therefore he cannot plead his case before him. The passage in 1 Timothy emphasizes that the arbitrator for whom Job asked has now been given, and he is a

E

man. In default of stronger evidence, it would seem reasonable to suggest that the passage in 1 Timothy does hark back to the passage in the Book of Job. We might suggest that whoever originally framed the formula which we find in 1 Timothy 2.5 read his scriptures in the LXX and not in the MT, for in two respects the LXX is more amenable to a christological interpretation than the MT. First, the LXX has ὁ μεσίτης ἡμῶν, which means literally "our mediator". We are justified in assuming that an early Christian would see this as a specific reference to Christ. The MT has only "There is no umpire between us".[7] Secondly, the LXX has modified the vivid metaphor that the Hebrew uses for the act of mediation: "who might lay his hand upon us both". As we shall be seeing in a moment, the thought of Christ as an umpire between God and men is sufficiently difficult, without having to envisage him as laying his hand on both the parties.

The word mesitēs stands out in this passage in Job all the more clearly for the fact that elsewhere in the LXX the verb yākhach (used in the Hiphᶜil) in the sense of "arbitrate" is normally translated by ἐλέγχειν and cognates, see Genesis 31.37 and Job 16.21. This latter passage is very relevant, as here also Job is pleading for arbitration between God and man. It is therefore very significant that the LXX in translating this verb in Job 9.33 has used two words μεσίτης καὶ ἐλέγχων. One is tempted to think either that the translator was nervous about using mesitēs in a case where God was one of the parties, and modifies it by the more familiar ἐλέγχων, or else (more likely perhaps) that καὶ ἐλέγχων is a gloss. In the latter case it is possible that these two words were absent from the LXX text of Job 9.33 used by the early Christian who originally composed the formula in 1 Timothy 2.5.[8]

No editor has connected the formula in 1 Timothy 2.5–6 with Job 9.32–3, though E. K. Simpson remarks, "Job's pathetic cry . . . has been answered."[9] As we shall be observing presently, there are dangers lurking in this simple notion of fulfiment. Several editors, however, point out the importance of ἄνθρωπος ("the man Christ Jesus"). G. Wohlenberg in 1906 suggested that the emphasis is on Christ's humanity over against Docetic tendencies,[10] and this is repeated by C. K. Barrett. Van Soden also sees a link here with Paul's doctrine of Christ as the Second Adam, a point underlined by J. N. D. Kelly, who welcomes it as an indication of Pauline authorship.

If we are to accept the suggestion that this passage is influenced by Job 9.32–3, it seems very likely that the early Christian who composed this formula looked on Job as an inspired prophet. This is not an attitude which is clearly reflected in the rest of the New Testament. It is true that in James 5.11 Job is held up as an example of patience, but explicit quotations from the book are very rare. Of the thirty-odd references in the "Index of Quotations" at the end of the Bible Societies' 1966 edition of the Greek New Testament,[11] the majority are echoes rather than citations, and some of them are very remote echoes indeed. There is, however, one early Christian writer who is an earnest student of the Book of Job, and that is Clement of Rome. In the sixty-five chapters of his Letter to the Corinthians he quotes Job no fewer than nine times.[12] Some of these are very long; in LVI.6, for example, he quotes the whole of Job 5.17–26. Clement obviously had a special interest in the Book of Job and a high regard for its chief character. In XVII.1–4, he is making the point that even the noblest characters in the Old Testament were modest men who admitted their own faults. He writes thus:

> Let us be imitators also of them which went about in goatskins and sheepskins, preaching the coming of Christ. We mean Elijah and Elisha and likewise Ezekiel, the prophets, and besides them those men also that obtained a good report. Abraham obtained an exceeding good report and was called the friend of God . . . Moreover concerning Job also it is thus written: *And Job was righteous and unblameable, one that was true and honoured God and abstained from all evil.*[13]

Lightfoot's translation brings out clearly the reference to Hebrews 11.39. So we learn from this passage that Job was worthy to stand in the list of the heroes of Israel given in Hebrews 11, and even that he may be reckoned by Clement among those who foretold the coming of Christ. Then in XXVI. 3, a free rendering of the LXX of Job 19.26 makes Job a prophet of the resurrection, the first time that he is so presented in Christian literature: "And again Job saith: *And Thou shalt raise this my flesh which hath endured all these things.*"[14] Finally we may note that in LVI.3, a series of citations from Psalms and Proverbs is introduced by the formula: "For thus says the holy word"; then follows in LVI.6: "And again it says . . ." with the long citation from Job 5 already referred to. So Clement looked on Job as "the holy word".

Now if we are right in our suggestion that the Pastorals are to be dated from about the middle of the first decade of the second century A.D., the fact that Clement of Rome takes such an interest in Job is very significant. As it is, scholars have often pointed out a number of parallels between Clement's Epistle and the Pastorals although the decision as to which is original depends for the most part on whether one accepts the Pauline authorship of the Pastorals or not.[15] At any rate, if one regards, for other reasons, the Pastorals as later than Clement, one can easily see how in the decade between Clement and the composition of the Pastorals an interest in Job as an inspired prophet could lead to the production of a formula such as we find in 1 Timothy 2.5-6. Certainly in that case we may say that the Pastorals and the Letter of Clement belong to much the same background, second generation Christianity, still in contact with Hellenistic Judaism, not with Palestinian Judaism. It is perhaps significant in this context that D-C described the words in 1 Timothy 2.6 as a Hellenized version of Mark 10.45.

The Rabbis, on the other hand, do not seem at all disposed to regard Job as an inspired prophet. There is much interesting speculation about the Book of Job to be found in the Tractate Baba Bathra in the Babylonian Talmud. It is quite clear that the Rabbis realized how rude Job was to God in his arguments, and they make no attempt to whitewash him. Commenting on Job 9.33 Rab remarks: "Dust should be placed in the mouth of Job: is there a servant who argues with his master?"[16] They also realized that, far from being a prophet of the resurrection, Job specifically denied it. We must, of course, make allowance for the fact that our Talmudic evidence is much later than the New Testament and the Rabbis' refusal to canonize Job as a saint may be influenced by the fact that the Christians were already claiming that prophecies of the resurrection of Christ, or the resurrection in Christ, were to be found in the book. But the rabbinic evidence does suggest very strongly that the Christian reliance on Job as a prophet of the resurrection originated in a Greek-speaking part of the Church. The MT of the Book of Job is obscure enough in all conscience, but it was sufficiently clear to prevent the Rabbis from doing what the LXX version did not prevent, drawing exactly the opposite conclusion about life after death from that intended by the author of the book. If, therefore, we are right in tracing 1 Timothy 2.5–6 back to Job 9.32–3, we are in contact not with rabbinic lore, but with Hellenistic speculation.

It should also be pointed out that if *mesitēs* in 1 Timothy 2.5 is used in the sense it bears in the LXX of Job 9.33, it commits the author of the Pastorals to a Christology which seems to lead ultimately to Arianism. "Job's pathetic cry . . . has been answered", writes E. K. Simpson, but what Job was asking for was an arbitrator who could lay his hand on the two parties. An arbitrator must, therefore, be neither God nor man. The only logical answer to Job's plea would be that given in the Testaments of the Twelve Patriarchs, an angel. It is by no means a coincidence that this solution is in fact suggested by Elihu in Job 33.23, and it is one of the arguments for the view that the Elihu chapters in the Book of Job are not from the pen of the author of the rest of the book. Philo's Logos, who is neither completely God nor completely man, would exactly fill the bill; and Philo's Logos is the true ancestor of the Arian Christ.[17] C. K. Barrett seems to be aware of this difficulty, for he points out that *mesitēs* is used in 1 Timothy 2.5 in a different sense from its use in Hebrews. In Hebrews the Son is not directly described as a mediator between God and man. He is the mediator of a new covenant. This means he is the agent and guarantor, not that he stands between God and man. It is significant that Moulton and Milligan given several instances of *mesitēs* being used in contemporary commercial and legal Greek in conjunction with a word for "guarantor".[18] At any rate, if *mesitēs* is connected with Job 9.33, we may say with confidence that we do not have a Pauline Christology here. D-C neatly points the distinction when he says that in this formula Christ is mediator because of his status and not because of his obedience, as in Philippians 2.1–11. It points, in fact, to a status-Christology rather than to a soteriological Christology.

We do not suggest, of course, that whoever first composed this formula was an Arian in intention. No doubt he composed it because he found what he thought was a prophecy of Christ's redemption in the Book of Job. Nor are we necessarily to imagine that it was the author of the Pastorals who composed this formula. On the contrary, it seems much more likely that the author is here reproducing material not his own. Cullmann maintains that the formula in 1 Timothy 2.5–6 was one of a number of bipartite formulas for use against paganism,[19] and he suggests that the mention of forgiveness in verse 6 indicates a baptismal context.[20] Possibly the use of the phrase "knowledge of the truth", ἐπίγνωσιν τῆς ἀληθείας, seems to point in this direction also. It seems to be used in reference to baptism in Hebrews 10.26.

There is, however, a further parallel with Clement's Epistle to the Corinthians which may throw some light on the background of 1 Timothy 2.5–6.[21] It is generally acknowledged that we have in Clement LIX—LXI some sort of a prayer used by Clement in public worship, though there is considerable dispute as to whether this can be called a eucharistic prayer (or part of a eucharistic prayer) or not.[22] When we compare the directions about public prayer given by the author of the Pastorals in 1 Timothy 2.1–4 with the actual prayer reproduced by Clement, we can point to a number of striking resemblances. On page 64 is a list of the parallels. Some of them, of course, are more striking than others. For example, the second last, the parallel between 1 Timothy 2.2 and Clement LXI.2, is not formally exact, for Clement prays that the rulers may behave in a peaceable and mild way, while the author of the Pastorals wishes Christians to be mild and peaceable. But nearly all the other parallels are very remarkable indeed. It is almost as if Clement were following a blueprint provided by the author of the Pastorals, though this, of course, would be a totally illegitimate conclusion to draw. The parallel does not leap to the eye at once because the Clementine prayer is so much longer, and also because the elements in the prayer are in a different order from what we find in 1 Timothy. But, if we were to eliminate the section relating to the forgiveness of sins in Clement LX.1–2, and the praises of God, consisting largely of echoes from the scriptures, in Clement LIX.3, we should have a prayer which conformed much more closely to what we meet in the 1 Timothy passage. The praises in Clement LIX.3 might be covered by the "thanksgivings" of 1 Timothy 2.1, and the prayer for forgiveness could conceivably be described as an "intercession", as prescribed in the same verse. The mediatorial function of Jesus Christ coming at the end of each passage is very remarkable. The "mediator" of 1 Timothy 2.5 is paralleled by the "high-priest and guardian" of Clement LXI.3. It greatly strengthens the supposition that the passage we have been discussing in this section is liturgical in origin.

In view of all this, it is by no means unjustified to suggest that in 1 Timothy 2.1–6 the author of the Pastorals is using an outline prayer for use in public worship. It is not the prayer itself. If we want to see what that is like, we must turn to Clement LIX—LXI. But he gives the traditional prayer-content. We may certainly conjecture that Clement's tradition and the tradition of the author of the Pastorals were the same, without in any way implying that one borrowed from the other. The prayer itself is a complex thing; when the author of the Pastorals does give us the actual wording he would use at the end, we find that it comprises at least two formulas, which have probably got different histories. That in verse 5 is probably more recent and suggests only a Hellenistic Jewish-Christian provenance. That in verse 6 is older and probably goes back to the Aramaic-speaking Church.[23] It is, therefore, quite certain that the author of the

Pastorals did not compose the formula in verse 6 himself, and it is most unlikely that he composed that in verse 5 either. Nor can we credit him with the invention of the prayer-outline which he provides in verses 1–6. Here, as in so many other places, he is reproducing his tradition, and we may well be grateful to him that he has told us so much about the liturgical tradition of one part of the Church, probably at the turn of the first century after Christ.[24]

TABLE 1

I TIMOTHY 2.1–6	I CLEMENT LIX—LXI
1. supplications	LIX.2. supplication
4. knowledge of the truth	knowledge of his glorious name
1. for all men	4. afflicted, humble, fallen, needy, ungodly, wandering, hungry, prisoners, sick, fainthearted
4. God desires all men to be saved	let all the nations know that thou above art God
1. for kings and all who are in high positions	LX.4. our rulers and leaders on the LXI.1. earth
3. this is good, and it is acceptable in the sight of God	
2. that we may lead a quiet and peaceable life, godly and respectful in every way	2. according to what is right and well-pleasing in thy sight administering in godly fashion the authority given to them by thee with peace and mildness
5. and there is one mediator between God and man, the man Jesus Christ.	3. through the high-priest and guardian of our souls, Jesus Christ.

6

Eve's Transgression:
1 Timothy 2.13–15

For Adam was formed first, then Eve; and Adam was not deceived,
but the woman was deceived and became a transgressor.
Yet woman will be saved through bearing children, if they continue[1]
in faith and love and holiness, with modesty.

The two great questions concerning this passage are: What is its
relation to 2 Corinthians 11.1–3,14 and what is its relation to
Jewish speculations about the nature of Eve's transgression? The
two are connected, of course. If we could be sure that Paul was in
touch with what at least later rabbinic tradition said about Eve's
transgression, it would not be difficult to fix the relation of this
passage to the passage in 2 Corinthians. In fact, however, many of
the elements which should help us to come to a conclusion are
uncertain, so that when we think we have got something definite,
we are in danger of finding that the whole question is just as open
as when we began. We do not know for certain, for instance,
what is the earliest mention of the *Haggada* on Genesis 3 with
which we are concerned; even if we could fix with any definite-
ness the date of what appears to be the earliest document that
witnesses to the *Haggada*, we cannot be sure that it has the same
implication as Paul's reference carries.

We may begin by clearing out of the way a few points that are
quite certain; there can be no doubt, for instance, that in Jewish
tradition before the time of St Paul women were regarded as
both inferior to men because created later, and as naturally more
gullible than men, two points made by the author of the Pastorals

here. The first point is proved by a simple reference to 1 Corinthians 11.8–12. Both S-B and Nauck[2] bring plenty of evidence to show that women were regarded as inferior. As for gullibility, this meets us as early as the Letter of Aristeas, where it is said of women that "they easily change their minds as a result of a specious argument".[3] Similarly Philo, discussing why the serpent speaks to the woman and not to the man, writes: "And woman is more accustomed to being deceived than man. For his judgement, like his body, is masculine and is capable of dissolving or destroying the designs of deception; but the judgement of woman is more feminine, and because of softness she easily gives way and is taken in by plausible falsehoods which resemble the truth."[4] But this, after all, is not so very remarkable; in any society where women are given a subordinate status and little education they acquire a reputation for gullibility.

The real question is: Does Paul, and after him the author of the Pastorals, reflect the tradition that Eve was actually seduced by the serpent in Eden, and therefore that her transgression was a sexual one? It is concerning this question that the evidence is so difficult to fix. Perhaps the best way of considering it is to cite the evidence for Haggada about Eve's transgression as far as possible in chronological order. We may divide it into seven sections, as follows:

1. *4 Maccabees 18.6–8.*
The mother of the seven martyred sons is represented as speaking thus to her family: "I was a pure maiden, and I strayed not from my father's house, and I kept guard over the rib that was builded *into Eve*. No seducer of the desert, no deceiver in the field, corrupted me; nor did the false, beguiling Serpent sully the purity of my maidenhood."[5] The Greek for "false, beguiling Serpent" is λυμέων ἀπάτης ὄφις. Townshend comments: "It seems hardly credible to us, but the Jews did actually believe that out in the desert there were demons who would lie in wait for women and lead them astray . . . And for the Jew the Prince of the demons was Satan, the λυμέων ἀπάτης ὄφις who had started his

campaign against mankind by corrupting Eve." There can be little doubt, therefore, that this passage betrays a knowledge of the tradition that the serpent had seduced Eve sexually. Unfortunately, it is not possible to date 4 Maccabees with any great accuracy. Townshend puts it between 63 B.C. and A.D. 38.[6] In F. L. Cross' *Dictionary of the Christian Church* it is merely put before A.D. 70.[7] It is interesting that this, probably the earliest reference to the tradition, should occur in a definitely Greek writing.

2. *Philo*

In the passage from *Questions on Genesis* which we have already quoted, Philo goes on to answer the question: Why did God first curse the serpent, next the woman, and then the man? He replies: "The arrangement of curses follows the order of wrong-doing. The serpent was the first to deceive. Second, the woman sinned, through him yielding to deceit. Third the man (sinned), yielding to the woman's desire rather than to the divine commands."[8] He then proceeds to offer an allegorical interpretation, so that reproduced here may well be the traditional one. It would seem to be a common-sense answer in any case. It looks quite like the midrash in 2 Timothy 2.13–15, for Philo does not say that the man was deceived, and there is emphasis on the fact that the woman was. There is no suggestion of seduction here, and it is interesting to note that Philo is anxious to avoid the notion of a curse on child-bearing, for he adds (section 49): "The experience [of child-bearing] comes to every woman who lives with a man. It is (meant) not as a curse but as a necessity." This is not the same as the "woman will be saved through bearing children" of the author of the Pastorals, but both he and the author seem to be anxious to obviate the notion of a curse.

Philo also discusses Genesis 3.16–19 in *Legum Allegoriae* III, a work which is really part of Philo's long, discursive commentary on the major part of the Book of Genesis. He works out in detail his allegory of Adam, Eve, and the serpent.[9] Adam represents intellect (*nous*), Eve represents sense-perception (*aisthēsis*), and the

serpent pleasure (*hēdonē*). Eating the fruit means the mind appre-
hending the object, and once sense-perception presents an object
for apprehension intellect must apprehend it. This is why Adam
had to eat the fruit when Eve gave it to him. In III, 64 he writes:
"for all deceit bears a very close resemblance to pleasure, and
pleasure is given by means of sense-perception", and in III, 66
Eve confesses that she has erred "through the deception of
pleasure, snake-like and fascinating as it is".[10] One can only say
that the tradition of the serpent's seduction of Eve would fit in
quite well with this, though it is not necessarily implied here. But
the question must arise, when one is dealing with so determined
an allegorist as Philo: Can one be sure that he thought that
anything had actually happened at all? He may have known the
tradition of Eve's seduction, but it is unlikely that he would
elaborate it, since his tendency is to say that Moses was not (here
at least) writing history, but that he was teaching moral philosophy by means of allegories.

We can, however, suggest with some confidence that the author
of the Pastorals knew of the passage in the *Questions on Genesis*,
a work which his unphilosophic mind would be more likely to
grasp than the more sustained exegesis of the *Legum Allegoriae*.
We certainly do not suggest that Paul had read Philo; it seems
very unlikely that Paul was influenced by him at all. But what is
peculiar to the author of the Pastorals in his exegesis of Genesis
3.16–19 is also found, in outline at least, in Philo. Here, we may
suggest, is one of the differences between Paul's treatment of
Eve's transgression and that of the author of the Pastorals.

3. Jewish Apocryphal Literature:
*The Books of Adam and Eve and the Apocalypse of Moses
and the Book of the Secrets of Enoch*

Here we are on very uncertain ground chronologically. Indeed,
this can be said of the two sources we have already quoted, for he
would be a rash man who would claim that 4 Maccabees is
certainly anterior to Philo. The first two books present slightly
different versions of the same legend. Wells believes that the

original tradition was Jewish, though it has been re-treated by both Christians and Gnostics.[11] He is inclined to put the earliest version of these writings early in the first century A.D. or even earlier, and he agrees with Kabisch that Paul in 2 Corinthians 11.1–3,14 may have been influenced by these writings, or by an earlier version of them.[12]

In *Vita Adae et Evae* 9—11 Eve is represented as doing penance after she and Adam had been driven out of paradise; she immerses herself up to the neck in the river Tigris. The devil, disguised as an angel, comes to comfort her and, persuaded by him, she comes out of the water: "and she fell on the earth and the devil raised her up and led her to Adam. But when Adam had seen her and the devil with her, he wept and cried aloud and said, 'O Eve, Eve, where is the labour of thy penitence? How hast thou again been ensnared by our adversary, by whose means we have been estranged from our abode in paradise and spiritual joy?' " This is not inconsistent with the idea of seduction, but does not necessarily imply it. In 16, the devil, describing his deception of Eve in the garden, says, "And with guile I cheated thy wife", which does not sound like seduction. Adam's complaint may only mean that Eve had been ensnared by the devil into leaving the water and thus ending a penance which, fully completed, might have brought relief.

In the Apocalypse of Moses 22 the devil is represented as taking the form of an angel. Eve bends over the wall of paradise and sees him. She lets him into the garden, and then follows a fairly straightforward account of the fall, except that after the devil had made Eve swear to give her husband the fruit to eat, we read (19.3): "And when he had received the oath from me (it is Eve's narrative), he went and poured upon the fruit the poison of his wickedness, which is lust, the root and beginning of sin, and he bent the branch on the earth and I took of the fruit and I ate." Wells thinks that this passage "points to the old idea of a literal seduction". It certainly does seem to imply that the first sin, which caused the fall, was lust not pride. But it cannot be said that it necessarily implies that the serpent seduced Eve.

What does seem to stand out, however, is that Paul in 2 Corinthians 11.14 betrays a knowledge of these writings or at least of their prototypes. In *Vita Adae et Evae* 9.1, before the devil appears to Eve at the Tigris, we read: "Then Satan was wroth and transformed himself into the brightness of angels, and went away to the river Tigris to Eve." In 2 Corinthians 11.1–3 Paul reminds the Corinthians that the serpent deceived Eve, and in verse 14 he says, "even Satan disguises himself as an angel of light". It is very difficult not to believe that Paul knew the tradition contained in these writings. An even clearer reference is found in a Jewish apocalyptic work belonging to the same tradition, The Book of the Secrets of Enoch or 2 Enoch. It is dated by Charles at about the beginning of the Christian era, and is only extant in Slavonic (Charles, op. cit., II, p. 425). In 31.6 it is written of Satan, "He conceived thought against Adam, in such form he entered [into Paradise] and seduced Eve, but did not touch Adam." This is the nearest verbal parallel to the Pastorals passage.

4. 2 Corinthians 11.1–3,14

> I wish you would bear with me in a little foolishness. Do bear with me! I feel a divine jealousy for you, for I betrothed you to Christ to present you as a pure bride to her one husband. But I am afraid that as the serpent deceived Eve by his cunning, your thoughts will be led astray from a sincere and pure devotion to Christ.

> And no wonder, for even Satan disguises himself as an angel of light.

The word for "deceived" in verse 3 is $\dot{\epsilon}\xi\eta\pi\acute{a}\tau\eta\sigma\epsilon\nu$. There is some doubt about the reading later on in this verse. The words "from a sincere and pure devotion to Christ" translate $\dot{a}\pi\grave{o}\ \tau\hat{\eta}s\ \dot{a}\pi\lambda\acute{o}\tau\eta\tau os$ $\kappa a\grave{\iota}\ \tau\hat{\eta}s\ \dot{a}\gamma\nu\acute{o}\tau\eta\tau os\ \tau\hat{\eta}s\ \epsilon\grave{\iota}s\ \tau\grave{o}\nu\ X\rho\iota\sigma\tau\acute{o}\nu..$ But $\kappa a\grave{\iota}\ \tau\hat{\eta}s\ \dot{a}\gamma\nu\acute{o}\tau\eta\tau os$ is missing from some important MSS and the editors of the latest Bible Societies' Greek New Testament put the words in square brackets. The chief difference they make is to emphasize the figure of sexual purity rather more.

Most editors agree, no doubt rightly, that Paul is using the figure of a betrothal here: Paul is the father. The Corinthian church is the bride, whom he has betrothed to Christ. The marriage is to be consummated at the Parousia.[13] But editors are much divided on the question whether Paul is aware of the tradition that the sepent seduced Eve. Schmiedel believes that such an idea is not impossible for Paul.[14] Plummer scouts the idea, saying that, if Paul had meant this, he would have said "by his lust ($\dot{\epsilon}\pi\iota\theta\nu\mu\dot{\iota}\alpha$)" instead of "by his cunning ($\pi\alpha\nu\nu\rho\gamma\dot{\iota}\alpha$)". Strachan writes: "There may be a reference to a rabbinical legend in *Haggada* that the serpent in Eden actually seduced Eve."[15] Allo emphatically denies that there is any reference to a seduction by the serpent, describing those who take this view as "syncretists".[16] He points out, as he is indeed entitled to do, that there is no explicit reference to a seduction in the Apocalypse of Moses or the *Vita Adae et Evae*. Héring seems to join the ranks of the "syncretists", for he writes: "The church which will be unfaithful is comparable to Eve seduced by the serpent (Gen. 3)."[17] He adds, "A different lesson is drawn from the defection of Eve in 2 Timothy 2.13–15", a point to which we shall be returning presently. It must be admitted that the metaphor which Paul uses is one of marriage and marital infidelity. We should not put too much emphasis on the details of the metaphor, as obviously Paul does not. But the balance of the evidence does seem to incline towards the view that Paul knew of the tradition that the serpent had seduced Eve, and assumes that his Corinthian readers will know it also. There is nothing surprising in this. 1 Corinthians 10.1–11 provides us with a very close parallel.

5. 2 Timothy 2.13–15

At first sight this passage would seem to furnish an argument for the Pauline authorship of the Pastorals, and it has been so used of course. Certainly the author agrees with Paul that woman's later creation implies the inferiority (or at least subordination) of women. Equally certainly, whoever wrote this passage knew of 2 Corinthians 11.1–3. Indeed, if the view taken throughout these studies is accepted, 2 Timothy 2.13–15 provides in fact the earliest attestation for 2 Corinthians, an Epistle which was not widely known in the period immediately after its writing. The Pastorals passage goes beyond what is said in 2 Corinthians 11.1–3 and adds three new assertions about Eve's transgression: (*a*) because of it women are more gullible than men; (*b*) Adam was not deceived; (*c*) women (without prejudice to the question of which women) may be saved through child-birth. There is no hint of these three assertions in Paul's undisputed letters. As has often been pointed out, Romans 7.11 would appear to be inconsistent with the second of them. And indeed the whole Pauline soteriology would seem very difficult indeed to reconcile with the third of these assertions.

The emphasis in the Pastorals passage is very much on the deception of Eve; Eve was deceived, but Adam was not. This is perhaps the place to look at the lexicography of the words for "deceive", ἀπατάω and ἐξαπατάω. The second word does not appear in the LXX, but is used in Herodotus of seducing a woman. ἀπατάω is of course the word used in the LXX of Genesis 3.13 "The serpent beguiled me and I ate". Moreover, it is the regular LXX translation of the Hebrew *pāthāh*, which in Pi'el means to seduce a virgin.[18] We have already noted the use of ἀπάτη in 4 Maccabees 18.8 for sexual seduction, the work of Satan. Oepke also quotes Susanna 56, where Daniel, accusing one of the two elders, says: τὸ κάλλος σε ἠπάτησεν, ἡ μιαρὰ ἐπιθυμία "her beauty seduced you, foul lust that it was". So the verb can be used of men being seduced sexually as well.

There is also some slight evidence that *parabasis* can have a specifically sexual meaning as well. S-B claims[19] that *'abhērāh*, which is its Hebrew equivalent, can mean specifically adultery in the Rabbis, and there are two interesting *scholia* in the LXX which may point in the same direction.[20] At 4 Kingdoms 2.24, the description of the children who were torn by bears after mocking Elisha, Codex A adds: τέκνα παραβάσεων καὶ ἀργίας "children of transgressions and idleness". This sounds like a suggestion that they were illegitimate, or at least of mixed parentage. The tendency of orthodox Judaism in the post-exilic period was to label Samaritans as illegitimate. If so, *parabasis* here means adultery. Similarly in Daniel 11.14 Codex E adds a descriptive phrase to the account of the Jews who sided with Antiochus IV, υἱοὶ τῶν παραβάσεων. This may be merely a Semitism for "law-breakers", but could just as well imply illegitimacy. It is possible therefore that the rather strange phrase in 1 Timothy 2.15 ἐν παραβάσει γέγονεν means more than merely that Eve broke the commandment not to eat of the tree in the midst of the garden. After all, Adam did this also, but the phrase is not used of him. It is more likely that it means "fell into sin", using "sin" in the Victorian sense of "living in sin". Grimm-Thayer class it with such phrases as γένεσθαι ἐν ἀγωνίᾳ, ἐν ἐκστάσει ["to be in agony, in an ecstasy"][21] and, even compare it with Romans 16.7: οἳ καὶ πρὸ ἐμοῦ γέγοναν ἐν Χριστῷ "who became Christians even before I did" (my tr.). The construction, they say, means "to come or pass into a certain state". This would certainly confirm the sense which we suggest here "she fell into a condition of sin".

On the other hand, Theodotion's translation used *parabasis* in its rendering of Genesis 3.17. It renders the Hebrew of "cursed is the ground because of you" as ἐπικατάρατος ἡ γῆ ἀδαμὰ ἐν τῇ παραβάσει σου, "cursed is the ground through 'your transgression' ".[22] It may be that the author of the Pastorals wrote ἐν παραβάσει γέγονεν because he had a text before him belonging to the same tradition as that which Theodotion used. If so, we must abandon the claim that *parabasis* in 1 Timothy 2.15 means sexual sin, as it is applied to Adam's sin also. This does not, of course, make it any the less likely that by ἐξαπατηθεῖσα the author means "having been seduced". Incidentally, if this connection were to be accepted, it would make it almost certain that the author of the Pastorals did not use the Hebrew text of Genesis.

At any rate we can say with confidence that B. S. Easton is quite unjustified in writing as he does: "This interpretation of Genesis 3.16 may be the Pastor's own, for no parallels have been found; the extracts cited by Billerbeck are as irrelevant as the legend that the serpent seduced Eve." It is true that "women will

F

be saved through bearing children" is the peculiar contribution of the author of the Pastorals, but it is not the case that the Haggadic evidence is irrelevant. Even Jeremias, who is jealous for the Pauline authorship, writes: "Here late Jewish ideas are taken over." D-C suggests that we do have the notion of the seduction of Eve here. He adds that, since Eve was seduced by the serpent, her Christian progeny must be saved by child-bearing, on the principle *quo quis peccat, eo salvatur*, which seems to sum it up very well. A number of editors would like to translate σωθήσεται δὲ διὰ τῆς τεκνογονίας as "she will come safely through the experience of child-birth", arguing that, according to the author, the curse of Eve is now removed through Christ. (So Bernard, Scott, Simpson, Barrett, N.E.B. margin, Phillips),[23] but Kelly is no doubt right in saying that this can only with difficulty be extracted from the Greek.

6. *Protoevangelium Iacobi*

Curiously enough, this is the earliest known passage where the serpent's seduction of Eve is absolutely explicitly referred to. It occurs in LIII.1: Joseph, on discovering that Mary is with child, exclaims: "Is not the story of Adam repeated in me? For as at the hour of his giving thanks the serpent came and found Eve alone and deceived her, so hath it befallen me also."[24] James says that the book is as old as the second century A.D., as it is mentioned by Origen. It seems to have an Alexandrian provenance. It is extant in the original Greek, and James maintains that "the author is not familiar with Jewish life or usages".[25] This may have some significance for the origin of the legend. There is no reason to think that there is any direct connection between the passage in the Pastorals and this work. We can say, however, that by the end of the second century A.D., the legend was known and accepted in certain Christian circles at least.

7. *Rabbinic Evidence*

In some rabbinic sources the legend took the form that the serpent seduced Eve and Cain was subsequently born as the fruit of this union. This would obviously have the added advantage from the Rabbis' point of view of explaining why God rejected Cain's offering in Genesis 4.5, an action for which no reason is given in scripture. The legend can be found in *Genesis Rabbah* 18. The references are given by H. St J. Thackeray: *Sota* 9b "The serpent, when he tempted Eve, said, I will kill Adam and take Eve to wife". *Ber. rabba* 18 "when the serpent saw how they [Adam and Eve] lived together as man and wife, then he lusted after Eve".[26] Neither of these references is earlier than the sixth century A.D. He gives the reference to the Cain legend as *Jalk. Schim. Beresch.* 42. Thackeray considers nearly all the passages set out in this chapter, but he does not discuss the possibility that Paul might not be responsible for the Pastorals. In the Babylonian Talmud we have a detailed account of how the serpent persuaded Eve to eat the fruit. Rabbi Hezekiah pointed out that in Genesis 3.3 Eve, in her conversation with the serpent, adds a prohibition which God had not actually uttered, "neither shall you touch it". The serpent thereupon pushed Eve against the tree, causing her to touch the fruit, and then said, "See, just as death did not ensue from the touch, so it will not follow from the eating of it."[27] The Rabbis are very far from supporting the view "woman will be saved through bearing children". Rabbi Johanan argued that the labour involved in providing food for man cost twice as much toil and suffering as that which a woman experiences in child-birth (this is proved by an elaborate play on words on Genesis 3.16–17).[28] He also claimed on the basis of Genesis 48.15–16 that it cost more to God to provide food for men than to save women in child-birth:

> the God who has led me [lit. "shepherded", hence "fed"] all my
>   life long to this day,
> the angel who has redeemed me from all evil.

A mere angel suffices to redeem from evil [including childbirth], it takes God to provide sustenance. Similarly there was a tendency to suggest that mothers of great men did not endure the pains of childbirth. For example, Rabbi Judah b. Zebina maintained that

Moses' mother had a painless delivery when he was born. He says: "Hence [it is learnt] that righteous women were not included in the decree upon Eve."[29] All this seems to point away from the passage in the Pastorals.

We ought now to be in a position to come to some conclusions about the passages in the New Testament concerning Eve's transgression. In the first place, it is very likely indeed that Paul knew the "angel of light" legend, and therefore that he knew the legend of Eve's seduction.[30] We may, therefore, interpret 2 Corinthians 11.1–3 as a reference to this seduction. From this it follows that the author of the Pastorals knew of this legend also, and is consciously referring to it in 1 Timothy 2.13–15. Here, however, the resemblance to the Pauline passage ends. Paul refers to the legend only *en passant*. He does not use it to prove any theological point. He uses it quite simply as an illustration to make clear the nature of his fears about the Corinthian church. This is all the more significant because we know from 1 Corinthians 10.4 that he can use midrash for doctrinal purposes. Here, however, he does not. He mentions the tradition and then passes on (though 11.14 shows that he still has it in mind a few verses later). The author of the Pastorals, on the other hand, uses the tradition in order to establish a number of theological principles which he no doubt considers important: the principle that women are naturally more gullible than men because Adam was not deceived, while Eve was; the principle that [Christian] women are redeemed from the curse by child-bearing and Christian behaviour. The first of these principles, we have noted, is not Pauline. Neither is the second: Paul would not have held that we are saved by anything which we do or suffer. Nor did he look on the *parabasis* as consisting in sexual sin, as apparently the author of the Pastorals does. For Paul the *parabasis* was disobedience, and the fact that he apparently accepted the legend of the seduction of Eve did not modify his view (see Romans 5.14). The author of the Pastorals nowhere shows his theological inferiority to Paul more clearly than in this passage.[31] No doubt those editors are right who see behind this passage a laudable desire to counter Gnostic tendencies to disparage marriage and procreation of children. But the way in which the author chose to do this has often had regrettable consequences on the thought of those theologians (and others) who regarded his work as genuinely Pauline.

One final point might be made: When and where did the legend of the seduction of Eve by the serpent originate? We do not know; but it may be that it originated in Greek-speaking Judaism, not in Palestinian Judaism. The LXX translates Genesis 3.13: "The serpent beguiled me" as ὁ ὄφις ἠπάτησέν με, and this is, of course, the text upon which the author of 4 Maccabees, Philo, Paul, the author of the Pastorals, and the author of the *Protoevangelium Iacobi* are all in their own various ways commenting. But the original Hebrew word is *hishshi'ani*, from the verb *nāshā'*, which in the Hiph'il means "deceive". Unlike *pāthāh*, however, this verb never means "seduce" in the sexual sense. The Greek verb ἀπατάω is used to translate both Hebrew verbs in the LXX. Is it not likely, therefore, that the transition from "deceive = beguile" to "deceive = seduce" was made in a Greek-speaking milieu? Slight supplementary evidence may be drawn from the fact that it would be easier for one brought up in a Greek cultural background to think of the root sin as being sexual (we remember Philo's equation of pleasure with deceit), and from the fact that the two clearest expressions of the tradition, that in 4 Maccabees and that in *Protoevangelium Iacobi*, are both contained in works originally written in Greek.[32] If this were the case, it would underline even more distinctly the difference between Paul's treatment of the legend and that of the author of the Pastorals, for Paul has explicitly rejected the conclusion that the first sin was sexual, while the author of the Pastorals seems to assume that this is so. In this respect as in many others Paul is nearer the tradition of Palestinian Judaism and the author of the Pastorals nearer to Hellenistic Judaism.[33]

7

Elements of a Baptismal Liturgy in Titus

The suggestion that we have in 1 Peter a baptismal liturgy is one that has been discussed by experts for the past fifty years. Conclusions vary from F. L. Cross' contention that we have a liturgy complete in everything except rubrics,[1] to C. F. D. Moule's denial that there is any more reference to baptism in 1 Peter than there is in most other letters in the New Testament.[2] More recently in the same journal A. R. C. Leaney has repeated the claim that there is in fact material from a baptismal liturgy in 1 Peter.[3] It seems to me that the publication by M.-E. Boismard of two articles in the *Révue Biblique* has greatly strengthened the case for the existence of a baptismal liturgy in 1 Peter.[4] His significance for our subject consists in the fact that he draws a close parallel between liturgical elements in 1 Peter and liturgical elements in Titus. This at once makes it likely that the author of 1 Peter and the author of Titus were using common liturgical material. This is, in fact, the conclusion to which Boismard comes. I will outline Boismard's conclusions, and then suggest some directions in which they could be amplified.

Boismard finds remarkable parallels between 1 Peter and Titus in two passages:

> 1 Peter 1.3–5 = Titus 3.4–7
> 1 Peter 1.13b–19 = Titus 2.11–14

On the opposite page we have written out the two passages in parallel, reproducing the Greek whenever there is a verbal or semantic coincidence.

TABLE 2

I PETER 1.3–5

Blessed be the God and Father of our Lord Jesus Christ! By his great mercy [κατὰ τὸ πολὺ αὐτοῦ ἔλεος] we have been born anew [ἀναγεννήσας ἡμᾶς] to a living hope [εἰς ἐλπίδα ζῶσαν] through the resurrection of Jesus Christ from the dead [δι' ἀναστάσεως Ἰησοῦ Χριστοῦ ἐκ νεκρῶν,] and to an inheritance [εἰς κληρονομίαν] which is imperishable, undefiled, and unfading, kept in heaven for you, who by God's power are guarded through faith for a salvation ready to be revealed in the last time.

TITUS 3.4–7

But when the goodness and loving kindness of God our Saviour appeared, he saved us, not because of deeds done by us in righteousness, but in virtue of his own mercy [κατὰ τὸ αὐτοῦ ἔλεος] by the washing of regeneration [διὰ λουτροῦ παλιγγενεσίας] and renewal in the Holy Spirit, which he poured out upon us richly, through Jesus Christ our Saviour [διὰ Ἰησοῦ Χριστοῦ τοῦ σωτῆρος ἡμῶν], so that we might be justified by his grace and become heirs in hope of eternal life [κληρονόμοι γενηθῶμεν κατ' ἐλπίδα ζωῆς αἰωνίου].

Boismard certainly seems to have a very strong case when we consider Table 2. The two passages are not, of course, word for word the same, but it does seem very likely that they own a common source. Boismard describes this source as a baptismal hymn. We must beware of attempting to distinguish too sharply between the various ingredients of early Christian worship. Scholars have identified in the New Testament early credal formulas, eucharistic prayers, catechetical material, homilies, as well as hymns and psalms. Two scholars, however, remind us to be cautious about such wholesale identifications. Thornton writes: "We possess no criteria at all for recognizing any record of a first-century baptismal service",[5] and Filson protests against the tendency to find poetry, whether Aramaic or Greek, concealed on every page of the New Testament: "Such brief snatches as 1 Timothy 3.16 may be better described as liturgical than as poetic, although the word liturgical may suggest to many a more highly developed ritual than the early Church actually had."[6] In fact, I suppose we know almost nothing at all about the actual ritual of the early Church, which may have been quite elaborate or very simple. However, it is as well to heed these warnings,[7] especially as, in the case of the 1 Peter passage under discussion here, there seems to be considerable disagreement among scholars as to what its character in the baptismal service originally was. Boismard, as we have seen, calls it a baptismal hymn, but F. L. Cross describes it as the bishop's solemn opening prayer. The author of the Letter to Titus has worked it into an exhortation to church leaders. Cross further complicates the matter by insisting that one cannot distinguish between a liturgy and a homily.[8]

When we turn to the passages given in Table 3, the parallel in language is not so close, but the parallel in thought seems to hold. In both passages, according to Boismard, we can see that the author of the Pastorals has modified the original more than the author of 1 Peter has done. He suggests that "a salvation ready to be revealed in the last time" is more primitive than the "he saved us" of the Titus passage. A difficult feature of Boismard's theory is the distance which separates the reference in 1 Peter to "God's

TABLE 3

I PETER 1.13b–19

Set your hope fully [τελείως ἐλπίσατε] upon the grace that is coming to you at the revelation of Jesus Christ [ἐν ἀποκαλύψει Ἰησοῦ Χριστοῦ]. As obedient children [τέκνα ὑπακοῆς] do not be conformed to the passions [ἐπιθυμίαις] of your former ignorance, but as he who called you is holy, be holy yourselves in all your conduct [ἐν πάσῃ ἀναστροφῇ]; since it is written: "You shall be holy, for I am holy." And if you invoke as Father him who judges each one impartially according to his deeds, conduct yourselves with fear throughout the time of your exile. You know that you were ransomed [ἐλυτρώθητε] from the futile ways inherited from your fathers, not with perishable things such as silver and gold, but with the precious blood of Christ, like that of a lamb without blemish or spot.

2.9 God's own people [λαὸς εἰς περιποίησιν].

TITUS 2.11–14

For the grace of God has appeared for the salvation of all men, training us [παιδεύουσα ἡμᾶς] to renounce irreligion and worldly passions [τὰς κοσμικὰς ἐπιθυμίας], and to live sober, upright, and godly lives [εὐσεβῶς ζήσωμεν] in this world, awaiting our blessed hope [τὴν μακαρίαν ἐλπίδα] the appearing of the glory [τὴν ἐπιφάνειαν τῆς δόξης] of our great God and Saviour Jesus Christ [σωτῆρος ἡμῶν Ἰησοῦ Χριστοῦ], who gave himself for us to redeem us [ἵνα λυτρώσηται ἡμᾶς] from all iniquity and to purify for himself a people of his own [λαὸν περιούσιον] who are zealous for good deeds.

own people" from the rest of the extract. In Titus "the people of his own" comes in close connection with the rest of the passage. It is also interesting to note that Titus apparently has "who are zealous for good deeds" in the place of 1 Peter's "that you may declare the wonderful deeds of him who called you out of darkness into his marvellous light", though the phrase in Titus might seem to find a parallel in 1 Peter 3.13, "if you are zealous for what is right".[9]

Boismard would make a distinction of function between the two passages where he finds common material. The first, he says, is a baptismal hymn (1 Peter 1.3–5 = Titus 3.4–7). The second he describes as baptismal catechesis (1 Peter 1.13b–19 = Titus 2.11–14). But the distinction seems a precarious one. In both writings the tone of both the extracts strikes one as lyrical, emotional, liturgical, rather than homiletic. This is more obviously true of Titus, where the resumption of the lyrical, liturgical vein in 3.4–8 is very marked after the plainly homiletic tone of 2.15—3.2. This makes one wonder whether the two extracts should be separated at all. May it not be that each author has divided what was originally one piece? In fact, when one comes to examine it, the material that each author has inserted in between the extracts is neither very extensive nor very obviously required by the structure of each writing. The author of 1 Peter has the larger element dividing the two; it falls into two parts, 1.6–9 and 1.10–13a. The first of these is no doubt appropriate to those to whom the Epistle is directed; they were living under the threat of persecution. The second part is a Christian midrash on the Old Testament, probably of the author's own composition, quite suitable for an epistle, but by no means in place in a baptismal service.[10] 13a is a transitional phrase. In Titus the material which separates the two passages is even more obviously of an *ad hoc* nature. 2.15 is a transition piece: 3.1–2, we shall be arguing later, is a traditional part of the baptismal service, but is certainly not to be connected with prayer or praise. The same could be said of 3.3, though it does not have any necessary connection with 3.1–2. Thus the question arises whether we should not regard the two extracts in both these New Testament writings as having originally made up one piece, a piece consisting of praise and prayer rather than of homily or catechesis.

Thus suggestion is confirmed by a comparison with a third writing in the New Testament, one which Boismard does not take into account, the Epistle to the Ephesians. The two relevant passages in the Epistle to the Ephesians are 2.1–10 and 5.25b–27. In Table 4 these two passages have been put beside the two passages from Titus with which we are concerned. When we look at the verbal parallels in Greek and also consider the parallels in thought, it is hard to resist the conclusion that there is a common source here. But the remarkable feature that stands out from this comparison is this: the author of the Epistle to the Ephesians does not seem to treat the source as consisting of two distinguishable elements, as the other two writers might be suspected of doing in view of the way they arrange their material. If we may for the sake of clarity label the first two passages pointed out by Boismard as A (1 Peter 1.35 = Titus 3.4–7) and the second as B (1 Peter 1.13b–19 = Titus 2.11–14), then it seems that the author of the Epistle to the Ephesians is using both A and B when he writes Ephesians 2.1–10. Most of this passage finds its parallel in Titus 3.3–7 (A), but "for we are his workmanship, created in Christ Jesus for good works" (Eph. 2.10) finds its closest parallel in Titus 2.14 "to purify a people of his own who are zealous for good deeds", which is B material. Similarly Ephesians 5.25b–27 finds its parallel partly in Titus 2.11–14 (B material), but its very explicit reference to baptism is paralleled in Titus 3.5–6, an A passage. Of course, it is not suggested that any of these writers was deliberately copying from the other; on the contrary, the evidence suggests not mutual borrowing but the use of a common source. The interesting feature of the Ephesian version of the common source is that it ignores the division. It seems to borrow indiscriminately from the A element and the B element. This suggests that in the common source the A element and the B element were not necessarily separate. Both probably formed one long item, whether an act of praise or prayer, we cannot say.

A comparison between 1 Peter 1.3–5 and Ephesians 2.4–10 yields interesting results: the verbal parallels are not particularly remarkable, but the parallel in thought content is clear:

PETER 1.3–5	EPHESIANS 2.4–10
ἔλεος	ἐν ἐλέει
ἀναγεννήσας	συνεζωοποίησεν
δι᾽ ἀναστάσεως	συνήγειρεν
διὰ πίστεως	διὰ πίστεως
φρουρουμένους	προητοίμασεν

The sequence of thought in both passages is almost identical: God of his great mercy has raised us up to a new life by the resurrection of Christ and we now by faith are well on the way to the consummation of that act of salvation. If we now call the two Titus passages into comparison again, we can see how the three authors have treated the same material. Titus appears in certain respects to be mid-way between the other two (this does not imply a judgement about chronology). Titus and Ephesians have reproduced the description of the former pagan condition more fully than has 1 Peter. 1 Peter refers to this only in 1.14, which does nevertheless preserve the word ἐπιθύμιαι common to all three writings. Similarly Ephesians and Titus have preserved the explicit reference to baptism.

TABLE 4

TITUS 3.3–8	EPHESIANS 2.1–10
3. disobedient [ἀπειθεῖς]	2. sons of disobedience [τοῖς υἱοῖς τῆς ἀπειθείας]
slaves to various passions and pleasures [δουλεύοντες ἐπιθυμίαις καὶ ἡδοναῖς ποικίλαις]	3. in the passions of our flesh, following the desires of body and mind, [ἐν ταῖς ἐπιθυμίαις τῆς σαρκὸς ἡμῶν ποιοῦντες τὰ θελήματα τῆς σαρκὸς καὶ τῶν διανοιῶν]
4–8. But when the goodness and loving kindness of God our Saviour appeared, he saved us, not because of deeds done by us in righteousness, but in virtue of his own mercy, by the washing of regeneration and renewal in the Holy Spirit, which he poured out upon us richly through Jesus Christ our Saviour, so that we might be justified by his grace and become heirs in hope of eternal life	4–10. But God, who is rich in mercy ... made us alive together with Christ (by grace you have been saved), and raised us up with him ... that ... he might show ... his grace in kindness towards us in Christ Jesus. For by grace you have been saved ... and this is not your own doing ... created in Christ Jesus for good works
ἡ χρηστότης	ἐν χρηστότητι
τοῦ σωτῆρος Θεοῦ ἔσωσεν ἡμᾶς	ἐστε σεσῳσμένοι
οὐκ ἐξ ἔργων	οὐκ ἐξ ἔργων
κατὰ τὸ πολὺ αὐτοῦ ἔλεος πλουσίως	πλούσιος ὢν ἐν ἐλέει
παλιγγενεσίας ἀνακαινώσεως	συνεζωοποίησεν συνήγειρεν
τῇ ἐκείνου χάριτι	χάριτι ἐστε σεσῳσμένοι

TITUS 2.11–14

For the grace of God has appeared for the salvation of all men, training us to renounce irreligion and worldly passions [κοσμικὰς ἐπιθυμίας] and to live sober, upright, and godly lives in this world, awaiting our blessed hope, the appearing of the glory of our great God and Saviour Jesus Christ, who gave himself for us [ὃς ἔδωκεν ἑαυτὸν ὑπὲρ ἡμῶν] to redeem us from all iniquity and to purify for himself a people of his own [καθαρίσῃ ἑαυτῷ λαὸν περιούσιον] who are zealous for good deeds [ζηλωτὴν καλῶν ἔργων].

EPHESIANS 5.25b–27

Christ loved the church and gave himself up for her [ἑαυτὸν παρέδωκεν ὑπὲρ αὐτῆς], that he might sanctify her, having cleansed her by the washing of water with the word [καθαρίσας τῷ λουτρῷ τοῦ ὕδατος ἐν ῥήματι], that the church might be presented before him in splendour, without spot or wrinkle or any such thing, that she might be holy and without blemish.

So far then we seem to have been led to envisage an original long baptismal prayer or act of praise known to all three authors, which they adapted to their own use independently of each other. It would be very rash to attempt to decide whether this was a written source or not. One might conjecture that it was not, since the elements in it can be treated so differently by the three writers concerned. It may simply have been the tradition of the long baptismal prayer belonging to the church in a certain area. All three documents with which we are concerned have connections with Asia Minor. The question arises: Does the interrelation end there? Or is it possible to trace a more extensive connection between the three Epistles? Many scholars have already traced materials common to these three Epistles either in the form of domestic codes or of catechetical instruction. Carrington, for example, has worked out what he believes to be the elements of a primitive Christian catechism in 1 John 3, nearly all of which could fairly easily be found also in Titus.[11] He does not draw the parallel with Titus, perhaps because of a desire to preserve the Pauline authorship of the Pastorals. Weidinger, who was the first to give close attention to the *Haustafeln* or domestic codes in the

New Testament, finds such a domestic code in Titus 2.1 ff.[12]
He remarks that the specifically Christian content is thinner than
in some of the other codes.[13] Similarly Selwyn lists Titus 3.5 in
Table V of his compilation of various codes, to be found in one
of the Appendixes to his edition of 1 Peter.[14] This table is called
"Baptism: its Nature Described". Parts of A and B in Titus
also appear in Table X, "Code of Subordination", and in Table
XII, "Slaves and Masters".[15] Thus Selwyn classifies the material
under review in Titus as either domestic codes or catechetical
material. He does not suggest the existence of a baptismal liturgy.

If, however, we widen our perspective, and look at the three
documents from the point of view of what contents they have in
common, it is possible to trace a quite distinct resemblance existing
between all three. In Table 5 overleaf I have drawn up a rough
list of contents for all three Epistles in parallel. In order to bring
out the resemblances, I have given a letter of the alphabet to each
subject; the two original extracts A and B are still designated by
these two letters, though it has been necessary to give them a
hyphen in Ephesians. I have preserved "good works" as a separate
element J, even though I have suggested above that it was originally an integral part of the baptismal prayer or act of praise. One
distinction between Ephesians and the other two Epistles at once
becomes apparent: whereas the other two have all their material
in common within a relatively short space, two chapters in Titus
and three in 1 Peter, in Ephesians the material is to be found in two
sections separated by a space of more than three chapters, a space
which comprises in fact the bulk of the Epistle. It is not possible
to trace with certainty an original order in which the various
elements held in common by these three Epistles must have
appeared. Indeed this comparison must put a question mark
against all attempts to recover a consecutive baptismal liturgy in
1 Peter. The three authors seem to have used the materials
common to the tradition very much as it suited them. We must
presently try to draw some conclusions from this, but first we
must attempt to relate the common pattern to the other Epistle in
which *Haustafeln* appear, Colossians.

TABLE 5

I PETER		TITUS		EPHESIANS	
1.3–5	A: liturgical piece	2.1–7	Right behaviour for various classes, including G women (2.3–5) H men (3.6)	2.1–3	C former pagan behaviour
1.6–12	[Midrash]			2.4–9	A–B liturgical piece
1.13—2.10	Instruction, including liturgical piece B which in its turn includes C former pagan behaviour[16] (1.14)	2.8	E the pagan critic	2.10	J good works
		2.9–10	F "slaves, be obedient and thus commend Christianity"	[2.11—5.21 Bulk of the Epistle]	
2.11–20	Exhortation, including D obedience to rulers (2.13–14)	2.11–14	B Liturgical piece	5.22–3	Theology of marriage, including
	E the pagan critic (2.15)	2.15	[Transition verse]	5.22–4	G Right conduct for women
	F "slaves, be obedient and thus commend Christianity" (2.18–20)	3.1–3	Exhortation, including D obedience to rulers (3.1)[17] C former pagan behaviour (3.3)	5.25	H Right conduct for men
2.21–5	[The Suffering Servant]	3.4–7	A: liturgical piece	5.26–7	A–B liturgical piece
3.1–6	G Right conduct for women	3.8	J good works	[6.1–4 Duties of parents and children]	
3.7	H Right behaviour for men			6.5–8	F "slaves, be obedient"
				[6.9 Duties of masters]	

Neither of the two passages in Ephesians in which we have found traces of the A-B source belongs to that part of the Epistle which is modelled directly on Colossians. This is particularly striking in the case of Ephesians 5.25b–27, which occurs in the middle of a passage that is modelled on Colossians; compare Ephesians 5.22—6.9 with Colossians 3.18—4.1. One can find occasional parallels to Ephesians 2.1–10 in Colossians; compare Colossians 1.21 and 2.12–13. The latter passage runs:

> You were buried with him in baptism, in which you were also raised with him through faith in the working of God, who raised him from the dead. And you who were dead in trespasses and the uncircumcision of your flesh, God made alive together with him, having forgiven us all our trespasses.

The verbal parallels here are συνήγειρεν, the phrase νεκροὺς ὄντας τοῖς παραπτώμασιν, and the unusual verb συνεζωοποίησεν. Certainly the author of Ephesians had Colossians in mind as he wrote this passage, but this does not suggest that the author of Colossians was acquainted with the common source which we have found behind Ephesians, 1 Peter, and Titus. When we look at Colossians in a wider perspective, we can trace some of the subjects dealt with in the other Epistles: there is "former pagan behaviour" (C) in Colossians 1.21; there is "right conduct for women" (G) in Colossians 3.18, and for men (H) in 3.19; and there is "slaves, obey your masters" (F) in 3.19–25. There is also a section on the duties of masters in 4.1 which is reproduced in Ephesians 6.9 and one on the duties of parents and children in Colossians 3.20–1 which is reproduced in Ephesians 6.1–4. All this seems perfectly consonant with the view that Colossians is Pauline, written at a period when the growing Christian communities were beginning to feel the need of *Haustafeln*; whereas Ephesians is deutero-Pauline, written at a time when the tradition of baptismal liturgy had developed further. The author of Ephesians is following Colossians fairly closely, but he is strongly influenced by the baptismal pattern which had grown up since the time of Paul.

G

Are we, after all, doing anything more than exploiting the acknowledged presence of *Haustafeln* in all four Epistles in order to build up a theory of a baptismal source common to three of them? I think that we can defend ourselves adequately from this charge by pointing to the specifically baptismal element which links together Ephesians, 1 Peter, and Titus, but which is absent from Colossians. In order to explain this, we must assume that by the time the latter three Epistles were written a *Haustafel*, or catechesis concerning household codes, was associated with the baptismal service. This is not to imply that when Colossians was written *Haustafeln* were wholly unconnected with baptism, but the connection is neither necessary nor particularly required in Colossians, whereas it is in the other three. We might even suggest that, if we may take 1 Peter 1.3—4.11 as forming the original core of the Epistle, there is a difference of form between Colossians and the other three Epistles. Colossians is written to a particular church to meet a particular situation. The other three are general Epistles, intended more as pastorals or church handbooks than as directives for any one situation. What the authors of Ephesians, 1 Peter 1.3—4.11, and Titus have done is to use the baptismal tradition of the church in their area to form the nucleus of a general pastoral letter. It is possible that in Colossians we can see this baptismal tradition in process of formation; but this does not mean that Colossians is the same sort of writing as the other three are.

As far as throwing light on the circumstances in which Titus was composed is concerned, the conclusions to be drawn are fairly obvious. The author of the Pastorals was in touch with the baptismal tradition of the church in Asia Minor. In his day liturgy as we know it today was only in process of formation: fixed formulas had not yet clearly emerged, but there was a traditional pattern which required certain elements to be present unfailingly. Actual verbal borrowing was possible, but the celebrant would feel free to use as much as he chose and to vary according to his own desire. It would be going beyond the evidence to suggest that the author of the Pastorals knew either 1 Peter or Ephesians as acknowledged Epistles. Walter Lock, in his introduction, gives a list of the parallels between Ephesians and the Pastorals; they are drawn either from the A–B passages which we have examined or are insignificant.[18] It would be more true to say that all three authors are roughly contemporary, writing within the same generation at least. One is naturally tempted to suggest that Ephesians is the earliest and that the author of 1 Peter is much closer to the creative sources of Christian theology than is the author of the Pastorals.[19] But the important distinction is between the Pauline period on the one hand and the period of, for example, the Epistle of Barnabas, the Didache, and the Shepherd of Hermas on the other. Titus, and therefore all the Pastorals, seems to be set firmly at the turn of the first century.

It may even be possible to suggest the source from which the A–B element in the baptismal tradition derives. This is, after all, the most stable element, one which comes nearest to being a fixed formula. Here if anywhere is the place where we are entitled to look for a derivation from older literature. In order to do so, however, we must make something of a detour. We must examine a passage in the First Epistle of John and compare it with the LXX of Psalm 130. My suggestion is that this Psalm was considered in the early Church to refer to Christian baptism and that John had this psalm in mind as he wrote this passage in his First Epistle. It has often been suggested that 1 John has baptismal connections; for example, T. C. G. Thornton agrees that there is baptismal language in the Epistle, though he maintains (rightly no doubt) that it is useless to try to trace a baptismal liturgy in it, as some have done.[20] C. H. Dodd finds references to baptism in 1 John 2.20 and 5.6.[21] Oscar Cullmann also sees indirect references to baptism in 5.6.[22] Table 6 overleaf provides a comparison between Psalm 130 (LXX 129) and 1 John 1.7—2.9. The LXX of Psalm 130 has been translated fairly literally, as a rendering of the MT would not bring out some of the significant points. On the surface, the resemblance is not striking, but the following points of contact may be indicated:

TABLE 6

PSALM 129 (LXX)

Out of the depths have I cried to thee,
Lord,
Lord, hear my voice.
Let thy ears be attentive
To the voice of my supplication.
If thou wert to mark lawless acts,
Lord,
Lord, who would endure?
For with thee is expiation [ἱλασμός].
For the sake of thy law have I waited
for thee, Lord,
My soul has waited for thy word.
My soul has hoped on the Lord.
From the morning watch till night.
From the morning watch let Israel
hope on the Lord.
For with the Lord is mercy,
And great redemption is with him,
And he shall redeem Israel
From all its lawless acts.
[λυτρώσεται ἀπὸ πάσων τῶν
ἀνομιῶν αὐτοῦ].

1 JOHN 1.7—2.5

... but if we walk in the light, as he is in the light, we have fellowship with one another, and the blood of Jesus his Son cleanses us from all sin [καθαρίζει ἡμᾶς ἀπὸ πάσης ἁμαρτίας]. If we say we have no sin, we deceive ourselves, and the truth is not in us. If we confess our sins, he is faithful and just, and will forgive our sins and cleanse us all from unrighteousness [καθαρίσῃ ἡμᾶς ἀπὸ πάσης ἀδικίας]. If we say we have not sinned, we make him a liar, and his word is not in us. My little children, I am writing this to you so that you may not sin; but if any sin, we have an advocate with the Father, Jesus Christ the righteous, and he is the expiation [ἱλασμός] for our sins; and not for ours only but also for the sins of the whole world. And by this we may be sure that we know him, if we keep his commandments. He who says "I know him" but disobeys his commandments is a liar, and the truth is not in him; but whoever keeps his word, in him truly love for God is perfected.

1. Psalm 130 is a psalm connected with the confession of sins. This passage in 1 John declares the importance of confessing one's sins more emphatically than any other passage in the New Testament.

2. Psalm 130 ends with the assurance that God will redeem Israel from all his lawless acts [ἀνομιῶν]. In 1 John 2.7,9, the author says that Jesus cleanses us from all sin [ἀπὸ πάσης ἀμαρτίας] or all unrighteousness [ἀδικίας]. In 1 John 3.4 ἀμαρτία (sin) is very explicitly identified with ἀνομία (lawlessness).

3. ἱλασμός, an unusual word in the Old Testament, and a unique word in the New Testament,[23] is common to both passages. John says that Jesus Christ is our ἱλασμός; he calls Jesus a Paraclete, and he says that we have this Paraclete "with the Father" (πρὸς τὸν πατέρα). This is very like the LXX of Psalm 130.4 παρά σοι ἱλασμός ἐστιν "with thee is expiation". When we bear in mind that in John 1.1 the Word is described as being "with God" (πρὸς τὸν Θεόν), it seems very likely that ἱλασμός in 1 John, referring to a person, Jesus Christ, means "expiation" rather than "propitiation". The latter meaning is defended by Leon Morris;[24] he maintains that it must mean "propitiation" in the New Testament, because, in the only two places in the LXX where ἱλασμός means "forgiveness" rather than "sin-offering", it is connected with the turning away of God's wrath. The two passages are this one in Psalm 130 and Daniel 9.19 (Theodotion's version). In both these passages (and in these only in the LXX) it translates the Hebrew sᵉlīchāh, a word which simply means "forgiveness" and does not really carry any necessary overtone of atonement. But if John identifies the ἱλασμός with Jesus, it seems necessary to take it in the sense of "means of forgiveness or expiation" rather than "means of propitiation" as Morris would have it. Otherwise the Father is represented as propitiating himself. The fact that ἱλασμός in the LXX can bear the meaning of simple forgiveness justifies us in concluding that its use in 1 John points to Psalm 130 rather than to such passages as Leviticus 25.9 or Numbers 5.8. An early Christian, reading in Psalm 130 "with

thee is ἱλασμός ", would naturally take it as a reference to Jesus Christ; and this conclusion fits in precisely with the sentence in 1 John 2.1–2: "we have an advocate with the Father, Jesus Christ the righteous, and he is the ἱλασμός for our sins".[25]

4. The LXX of Psalm 130.5–6: "My soul has waited for thy word" may be echoed in 1 John 2.5, "whoever keeps his word". At least an early Christian might see the phrase in the Psalm as the utterance of one who was expecting the coming of the Word.

I am not suggesting that anything like a liturgy of baptism based on Psalm 130 lies behind this passage in 1 John. But it may be suggested that the author of 1 John was familiar with the use of Psalm 130 in a baptismal context and that it naturally coloured his words when he was writing what is perhaps a baptismal homily. When one considers Psalm 130 in this light, one sees how very appropriate it would be for baptism from the point of view of early Christians. In verse 1 those who are to be baptized cry from the depths. This would correspond with the confession of sins that had to precede baptism, and to the depths of water in which they were to be immersed. Then follows in verse 3 a reference to sin confessed and to the redeemer (ἱλασμός, identified by John with the Paraclete who is with the Father). They wait for God's word. This word is perhaps the baptismal formula. In verse 6 they are described as waiting "from the morning watch". We know that by the end of the second century it was customary to perform adult baptisms very early in the morning. F. L. Cross conjectures that in 1 Peter we have a liturgy for the paschal vigil, so he sees nothing anomalous in the suggestion that within New Testament times baptism was performed early in the morning.[26] Finally, in verses 7–8 come references to the redemption which is brought to the newly baptized by the "one baptism for the remission of sins". It is worth pointing out also that in 1 John 1.5–7 we have light-and-darkness language which may well have a baptismal reference.[27]

The Epistles of John are widely regarded as directed to churches in Asia Minor. It is with Asia Minor that all three Epistles are connected in which we have found traces of the common baptismal tradition, and in particular of the baptismal prayer or act of praise which we have called A–B. If the author of the Johannine Epistles knew of the use of Psalm 130 in his baptismal tradition, it would not be surprising that the same Psalm should, to some extent at least, lie behind the baptismal tradition of these three Epistles. When we consider the A–B element with this in view, we can point to certain connections: Titus 2.14 has ἵνα λυτρώσηται ἡμᾶς ἀπὸ πάσης ἀνομίας ("to redeem us all from all iniquity"), which is very close indeed to Psalm 130.8 λυτρώσεται τὸν Ἰσραὴλ ἐκ πασῶν τῶν ἀνομιῶν αὐτοῦ ("he will redeem Israel from all its lawless acts"). Compare also 1 Peter 1.18, ἐλυτρωθῆτε. Then the word ἔλεος "mercy" is common to all three Epistles (Eph. 2.4; 1 Pet. 1.3; Titus 3.5) and occurs in Psalm 130.7. Thirdly, Psalm 130 has two references to hope: "my soul has hoped on the Lord" and "let Israel hope on the Lord", and in 1 Peter 1.3 we have the reference to the "living hope"; the note of hope is also found in Titus 3.7, "heirs in hope of eternal life"; see also Titus 2.13, "awaiting our blessed hope". It is also possible that Psalm 130 throws light on that puzzling phrase in Ephesians 5.26: "having cleansed her with the washing of water with the word [ἐν ῥήματι]". What word? Perhaps it is inspired by Psalm 130.5 (LXX): "My soul has waited for thy word". LXX has λόγος but Aquila translates with ῥῆμα. Perhaps the word is the baptismal formula for which the candidate for baptism has been waiting so eagerly. Christ is regarded as the minister of baptism, the Lord of whom the Psalmist speaks. In Ephesians, the whole Church is baptized primarily by Christ's act of self-giving in the cross and resurrection, but this is represented and fulfilled in every Christian baptism.[28] Incidentally, it is remarkable that the parallels to Psalm 130 come from both A and B elements, another indication that A and B were originally one piece.

Taken singly, none of these connections would be very remarkable, but taken all together they have a certain force. At any rate, if there is an A–B source behind the three Epistles in question, the Old Testament is by far the most likely place to which to turn for its original inspiration. It cannot be taken as proved that Psalm 130 must have been the inspiration behind this source, but it is at any rate the right sort of direction in which to look. The possible connection of Psalm 130 with 1 John makes one wonder whether this Psalm may not also have provided the starting-point for the most definite element in the baptismal tradition which we have found to be common to Ephesians, 1 Peter, and Titus.

8

Eucharistic References in 1 and 2 Timothy

This title begs the question, for several editors have remarked on the absence of references to the eucharist in the Pastorals. A comparison with the Didache, however, gives grounds for believing that in fact there are such references in 1 and 2 Timothy, not because the author of the Pastorals had any particular teaching to give concerning the eucharist, but because he seems in places to be quoting from a eucharistic prayer. Before we institute the comparison, however, it is necessary to reach some conclusions about the date of the Didache itself. This is not something which can be taken for granted today. When it was first discovered, the tendency was to put it very early indeed, perhaps before the end of the first century. Then came a reaction: in his important book on the subject F. E. Vokes suggested in 1938 that the Didache was a work of the second half of the second century, that the apparently primitive features were, in fact, deliberate archaisms, and that it was evoked by the rise of Montanism.[1] His view is that "it gives in the form of a summary of apostolic teaching a description of what can be called the 'apostolic element' of Montanism, and that its purpose is the defence of the 'New Prophecy'".[2] In the last twenty-five years, however, the tendency has been to regard the Didache as genuinely primitive, not archaistic, though few, if any, would follow Audet in putting it in the seventh or eighth decade of the first century.[3] B. C. Butler has argued that as far as the source known as "The Two Ways" is concerned, the Didache is dependent on the Epistle of Barnabas.[4] Perhaps a more likely view is that both are dependent on a common source, especially as what is apparently a Jewish version of "The Two Ways" has now turned up among the Qumran documents. The position is well expressed by Altaner, who says that a date after A.D. 150 is very unlikely, and who suggests the use of a common source by the Didache and the Epistle of Barnabas.⁵ R. Glover is impressed by the view which would not put the Didache any later than the Shepherd of Hermas.⁶

Assuming then, provisionally at least, that we may put the Didache somewhere between A.D. 120 and 150, we may proceed to a comparison of it with certain passages from the Pastoral Epistles. In Table 7 are drawn up in parallel two passages from the Pastorals and two from the Didache.⁷ The parallel here is impressive without in the least suggesting, as Vokes believes, that the author of the Didache has simply copied from the Pastorals. It looks very much as if the two authors were quoting a common source. All the elements in 1 Timothy 4.3–5 are found in chapters 9 and 10 of the Didache, though in a different order and sometimes with variant phraseology: God's creation of food for men, with which the author of the Pastorals begins, is found in Didache 10, which makes explicit what is implicit in the Pastorals, that he makes it for men's enjoyment. The 1 Timothy passage goes on to say that those who believe and fully know the truth receive God's gifts with thanksgiving. The thought of knowledge is echoed in Didache 9, and knowledge and faith come together in Didache 10. In 2 Timothy 1.10 comes the reference to life joined with immortality (better perhaps "incorruptibility") and this finds a parallel in Didache 9 ("life and knowledge") and even more exactly in Didache 10, where we have both "immortality" [ἀθανασία] and a reference to the eternal life which comes with the spiritual food and drink. Finally, though there is no explicit reference to the consecration of the gifts by the word of God and prayer in the Didache, this is in fact implied by the context of the two prayers, which are cited in order that they may be uttered over the cup and the broken bread. I am sure that, if the references in the Pastorals did not occur in such a very uneucharistic

TABLE 7

I TIMOTHY 4.3-5

... who forbid marriage and enjoin abstinence from foods which God created [ἔκτισεν] to be received with thanksgiving by those who believe and know the truth [τοῖς πιστοῖς καὶ ἐπεγνωκόσιν τὴν ἀλήθειαν]. For everything created by God is good, and nothing is to be rejected if it is received with thanksgiving [μετ᾿ εὐχαριστίας] for then it is consecrated by the word of God and prayer [ἁγιάζεται γὰρ διὰ λόγου Θεοῦ καὶ ἐντεύξεως].

2 TIMOTHY, I.IO

... and now has manifested through the appearing of our Saviour Christ Jesus, who abolished death and brought life and immortality to light [φωτίσαντος δὲ ζωὴν καὶ ἀφθαρσίαν] through the gospel.

DIDACHE 9

Concerning the eucharist [τῆς εὐχαριστίας], give thanks in this manner; first we give thee thanks, holy Father, for thy holy vine of David thy Servant [τοῦ παιδός σου], which thou hast made known to us through Jesus, thy Servant [τοῦ παιδός σου]. To thee be glory for ever. Concerning the broken bread: we give thee thanks, our Father, for the life and knowledge [ζωῆς καὶ γνώσεως] which thou hast made known to us through Jesus thy Servant [τοῦ παιδός σου]. To thee be glory for ever.

DIDACHE IO

But after being filled give thanks thus: we give thee thanks, holy Father, for thy holy name which thou hast caused to tabernacle in our hearts, and for the knowledge and faith and immortality [τῆς γνώσεως καὶ πίστεως καὶ ἀθανασίας] which thou hast made known to us through Jesus thy Servant [τοῦ παιδός σου]. To thee be glory for ever. Thou, almighty despot, hast created [ἔκτισας] all things for the sake of thy name, and thou hast given food and drink to men for their enjoyment, that they may give thanks to thee; but on us thou hast bestowed spiritual food and drink and eternal life through thy Servant [τοῦ παιδός σου].

context, the remarkable parallel with the language of the Didache would have attracted more notice.

Before we attempt to draw out the implications of this, however, we should give some attention to the very various opinions which are held about the significance of chapters 9 and 10 of the Didache. There has always been a tendency, ever since the Didache was discovered, to assign chapter 9 as a prayer for the agapē and to reserve chapter 10 as a prayer for the eucharist. This has the weighty authority of Lietzmann,[8] though he maintains that the two were not separate when the Didache was written. Drews varies this by suggesting that chapter 9 gives us the prayer for an unofficial weekday agapē, and chapter 10 that for an official Sunday eucharist.[9] But can we be so sure that the agapē and eucharist were completely separate when the Didache was written? It depends when one believes it was written, but it would be rash to suggest that they were completely separate before the second half of the second century. Perhaps Pliny's evidence shows that they were separable, but even this is by no means clear. Vokes goes further and maintains that both prayers were intended for use in the agapē;[10] but we must bear in mind that, according to him, they are both intended as archaizing reconstructions of the usage of an earlier day, and do not therefore give us direct evidence about contemporary usage. Daniélou, who holds that these prayers are very early indeed, believes that they reflect a period when the eucharist took place in the context of a meal, and that therefore the repetition of thanksgivings such as we find in the Didache is perfectly natural, since they reflect Jewish usage at religious meals. See *La Théologie du Judéo-Christianisme* (p. 387). This view has much to commend it. Interesting also is Erik Peterson's reconstruction of Didache 9.2–3 and 10.2–4 so as to form a very primitive hymn intended for use at the fraction. See his article "Didache cap. 9 e 10" in *Ephemerides Liturgicae*, January–December 1944 (pp. 3–13). He believes that this hymn was later used in the agapē and that this is its purpose in the Didache. Alfred Adam on the other hand (art. cit.) claims that the prayers in chapters 9 and 10 were originally intended for the agapē and not for the eucharist. Much has been made of the "bread scattered upon the mountains"; it has been claimed that this points to a Judean provenance. This has been denied, and the mountains explained as either an eschatological feature (they were to be made level at the Parousia), or the whole phrase has been linked with John 6.1–15.[11] We must remember the point well expressed by Richardson:[12] "Yet it is indisputable that the Didache calls the rite a eucharist; and there is no justification for explaining the term away as here meaning a quite general thanksgiving,[13] or for assuming that the real eucharist followed but was left undescribed for motives of secrecy." We might put the difficulty in other words by saying that chapter 9 describes the prayer as a prayer for the eucharist, while chapter 10 gives what is a much more eucharistic prayer.[14] The solution might be along the line of regarding chapters 9 and 10 as alternative eucharistic prayers, a view put forward sixty years ago by Batiffol.[15] Woolley follows this line, and suggests that the two prayers were based on the two prayers for use before and after meals respectively which are recorded in the Mishna.[16]

Part of the difficulty lies in the fact that the earlier one places the Didache, the more difficult it is to suppose that agapē and eucharist were separated. The choice seems to be between two courses: *either* we put the Didache very early indeed (following such scholars as Audet and Adam), in which case it is precarious to distinguish agapē from eucharist;[17] *or* we put it later, perhaps as late as A.D. 130, and hold that in chapters 9 and 10 we have very primitive eucharistic prayers adapted for use at the agapē (as Peterson and perhaps Gibbins). It must be said that O. Cullmann's reconstruction of the liturgy at the end of chapter 10 is most convincing,[18] and it is very difficult to imagine that this could have taken place anywhere else than at the eucharist. The liturgy ends with the sacred formula "Maranatha"; then would naturally follow the communion. Perhaps this is the point where the inspired prophets would utter their message. At any rate, in this study we proceed on the assumption that the tradition represented in the Pastorals is early enough to be considered as definitely eucharistic.

In the Pastorals, then, we may claim that we can trace some elements of a eucharistic prayer. But what exactly did the eucharist comprise in the period when the Pastorals were written? It can hardly be said that there is a universal agreement among scholars about the origin of the eucharist, but at least one influential scholar holds that it derives from the Jewish custom of invariably pronouncing a blessing over meals. Indeed the great majority of commentators on 1 Timothy 4.3–5 have assumed without argument that the reference is here only to grace before meals. The only apparent exception is D–C where there is some suggestion that the eucharist might be in mind.[19] A weighty authority on the other side is G. A. Michell, who argues that the original idea in the consecration of the eucharist was that the thanksgiving uttered over the elements itself consecrated them.[20] This was derived from the Jewish belief that to utter a thanksgiving for food over the food sanctified the whole meal. Only later, he claims, did the idea of imposing the name come in: "By the end of the second century (A.D.) the Rabbis were teaching that *berakoth* owed their efficacy to the first clause, which was understood to put the 'Name' upon the object over which it was pronounced."[21] In other words, the notion that the uttering of the name was the act of consecration is later. He supports this by referring to Justin's account of the eucharist, where there is no mention of uttering the name, but the elements are consecrated by being "eucharistized". Justin, he says, uses the "Name-consecration" in baptism, which makes its absence in the eucharist all the more striking. Justin does refer to the Christian habit of giving thanks for food; but, says Michell, he obviously distinguishes this food from the eucharist on the grounds that over this food Christians utter a thanksgiving for creation, whereas over the eucharist they offer a thanksgiving for redemption. On these assumptions, therefore, the 1 Timothy passage does not refer to the eucharist, but to grace before meals. This argument has received the approval of Professor J. G. Davies recently.[22] It is worth pursuing, because it brings us to an examination of Justin, who, I believe, can give us light on this passage in 1 Timothy 4.

Michell's argument is that Justin distinguishes between blessings uttered over food by Christians and the blessing uttered over the bread and wine in the eucharist. But when we examine the two passages on which this view is based, they do not seem to bear this conclusion out. The first is Apology 13.1,9:[23]

Since we are not atheists, we worship the creator of the universe and claim, as we have been taught, that he has no need of blood-offering and libations and incense; and we praise him as far as we are able with the word of prayer and thanksgiving [λόγῳ εὐχῆς καὶ εὐχαριστίας] uttered over all our contributions; for we have traditionally held that the only honour worthy of God consists, not in wasting in fire things given by him for our support, but rather in using them for our benefit and the benefit of those who are in need.

The contrast here is between pagan or Jewish worship on the one hand and Christian worship on the other. Blunt comments on this passage: "There may be an allusion to the eucharistic distributions to the poor." This, I believe, is the right solution: at the eucharist Christians bring the bread and the wine and their alms to be blessed by God. It is not an allusion simply to grace at meat. The second passage occurs in Apology 67.2: "And over all our contributions we bless [ἐπὶ πᾶσι δὲ οἷς προσφερόμεθα εὐλογοῦμεν][24] the maker of all things, through his Son Jesus Christ and through the Holy Spirit." This passage occurs between the two descriptions of the eucharist which Justin gives. He is comparing worship with worship. A comparison of pagan and Jewish public worship with grace said by Christians before meals would not serve his purpose.

When we turn to the passages where Justin describes the eucharist, we find quite a remarkable parallel to the Pastorals. In Apology 66.2 he describes the consecrated bread as "the food over which thanks has been given by that word of prayer which comes from Christ [τὴν δι'εὐχῆς λόγου τοῦ παρ' αὐτοῦ ⟨sc. Χριστοῦ⟩ εὐχαριστηθεῖσαν τροφήν]". This is distinctly reminiscent of the phrase in I Timothy 4.5: "it is consecrated by the word of God and prayer [διὰ λόγου Θεοῦ καὶ ἐντεύξεως]". In

Apology 66.1 we read, "And this food is called by us *eucharistia*, which no one is allowed to share except him who believes that our teachings are true and has been washed in the bath which is for the remission of sins and regeneration." [λουσαμένῳ τὸ ὑπὲρ ἀφέσεως ἁμαρτιῶν καὶ εἰς ἀναγέννησιν λουτρόν]. This could almost be a paraphrase of 1 Timothy 4.3: "to be received with thanksgiving by those who believe and know the truth", especially if, as we shall be suggesting later, the phrase "know the truth" may in itself carry overtones of baptism. Nor can we fail to notice the resemblance of Justin's phraseology to the sentence describing baptism in Titus 3.5: "by the washing of regeneration" (διὰ λουτροῦ παλιγγενεσίας]. It is not to be imagined, of course, that Justin is either deliberately quoting the Pastorals or consciously modelling himself on them. Such an idea would be absurd in this context of the Apology. What does seem to be present is a common source, a common eucharistic and perhaps baptismal tradition.

I suggest therefore that Justin's phrase τὴν δι᾽ εὐχῆς λόγου τοῦ παρ᾽ αὐτοῦ εὐχαριστηθεῖσαν τροφήν affords an adequate explanation for the phrase in 1 Timothy 4.5 which has puzzled commentators so much: διὰ λόγου Θεοῦ καὶ ἐντεύξεως. It is not the Word himself;[25] nor is it God's word in Genesis 1.31: "Behold, it was very good."[26] It is not even the blessing of food generally in the name of God.[27] The word of God is Jesus' word "Do this", or else the formula of administration "Take, eat". The fact that the author of the Pastorals calls this the word of God is not a very great obstacle: he is quite capable of describing Jesus as God; see Titus 2.13 and compare 2.10, "the doctrine of God our Saviour". The ἔντευξις would be the eucharistic prayer itself. The author of the Pastorals is therefore making the point in 1 Timothy 4.1–5 that we have no right to reject bread or wine as unfitted for our use, because God himself in Christ has sanctified these elements for our special use in the eucharist, very much the same point as is implied in Didache 10, where the prayer says that God has given food for the use of all men, but spiritual food for the special use of Christians in the eucharist. It may be that the *disciplina arcani* has influenced the author of the Pastorals to the extent that his language is rather more general than that of either the Didache or Justin, but the eucharistic reference is surely unmistakable in the background.

We should also point out that Justin, far from sharply distinguishing between thanksgiving for creation and thanksgiving for redemption, as Michell maintains, associates both with the eucharistic thanksgiving. It is worth noting in this connection that in Apology 61.8 Justin explains that Christians worship on a Sunday both because God created the world on that day and because on that day Christ rose from the dead. But the more explicit statements are found in his Dialogue with Trypho; in Dialogue 41.1 he writes of what we do in the Eucharist thus: "We give thanks to God at the same time for his creation of the world with all that is in it for man's sake, and because he has freed us from the evil in which we were born, and has completely destroyed the powers and authorities . . . etc."[28] Justin then quotes the well-known passage from Malachi 1.10–11 about the pure offering, and claims that it is fulfilled in the Christian eucharist as contrasted with the Jewish offerings that were being constantly offered at the time when Malachi wrote.[29] We may note, incidentally, Justin's admirable emphasis on the priestly nature of the worshipping community: it is we who give thanks in the eucharist. Later on in Dialogue 116.3 he claims that the vision of the High Priest Joshua described in Zechariah 3 is a prophecy of the priestly body, the whole Christian Church as found in Christ: "We are the true high-priestly race . . . God will accept sacrifices from the hands of none but those who are his priests." Finally, we may refer to Dialogue 117.1: "From of old God has been witnessing that all these sacrifices are pleasing to him which are offered through that name which Jesus Christ instituted, that is, at the thanksgiving for the bread and the cup, which are celebrated by the Christians in every part of the earth".[30] Thus Michell's appeal to Justin in order to reinforce the view that *eucharistia* could mean merely thanksgiving over meals is not really borne out by the evidence. The strictly eucharistic reference remains. In addition,

H

the prominent position of the name in this passage would seem to militate against Michell's theory.

So far we have not devoted much attention to 2 Timothy 1.10 except to point out that it has its parallel in both the prayers found in the Didache. This is not without significance, for it suggests that a reference to what we today would call the two sacraments was a normal part of the eucharistic prayer. There is some evidence that the words ἐπίγνωσις τῆς ἀληθείας (or the cognate verb ἐπιγινώσκω), "knowledge of the truth", could refer to baptism even within the pages of the New Testament. See Hebrews 10.26: "If we sin deliberately after receiving the knowledge of the truth [τὴν ἐπίγνωσιν τῆς ἀληθείας] . . .". Compare also 1 Timothy 2.4 "[God] desires all men to be saved and come to the knowledge of the truth." J. Dupont in Gnosis (p. 33) suggests that in Colossians εἰς ἐπίγνωσιν carries a baptismal overtone. Thus τοῖς πιστοῖς καὶ ἐπεγνωκόσιν τὴν ἀλήθειαν ("those who believe and know the truth") may well mean "those who have confessed their faith in baptism". Hermas also seems to use *epiginōskō* in this sense; see Similitudes 9.XVIII, 1: "How, Lord, I said, can they have become worse if they have received full knowledge of God?" [Θεὸν ἐπεγνωκότες].[31] The author of the Shepherd of Hermas was, of course, very much concerned about the problem of post-baptismal sin.

Together with "knowledge", "life" is also associated with baptism, and as well as "life" we find the thought of immortality (ἀθανασία) or incorruptibility (ἀφθαρσία). Thus Didache 9 couples together life and knowledge, while Didache 10 gives us knowledge, faith, and immortality. This sort of language is certainly found in Ignatius; see Ephesians XVII: "Why do we not all become wise, since we have received the knowledge [γνῶσιν] of God, which is Jesus Christ? Why do we stupidly go to ruin, ignoring the free gift [χάρισμα] which the Lord has truly sent us?"[32] Then in Ephesians XX follows the famous reference to the eucharist: ". . . breaking the one loaf, which is the medicine of immortality, the antidote against dying [φάρμακον ἀθανασίας, ἀντίδοτον τοῦ μὴ ἀποθανεῖν], guarantee of eternal life in Jesus

Christ". These two passages would seem to give us a reference to both baptism and the eucharist in this passage. Thus it is not far-fetched to suggest that the phrase in 2 Timothy 1.10: φωτίσαντος δὲ ζωὴν καὶ ἀφθαρσίαν ("brought life and immortality to light") is a reference to baptism and the eucharist which is in fact derived from a eucharistic prayer. The association of light with baptism is traced by some in the New Testament itself (see our reference to 1 John 1.5–7 on p. 94 above). Spicq, who considers that 2 Timothy 1.9–12 is liturgical, refers to Hebrews 6.4, 10.32, both passages in which φωτισθείς very probably refers to baptism. In Justin's Apology 61.2 we read: "This washing [λουτρόν] is called enlightenment [φωτισμός]", in 65.1 the baptized person is described as "the enlightened one", ὁ φωτισθείς.

Two other parallels are worthy of consideration. The first is 1 Clement LIX.2, already briefly referred to in Chapter 7, note 27 (p. 132 below). It occurs at the beginning of what is often regarded as an extract from a liturgical prayer, and runs thus:

> The creator of all things through his beloved servant [παῖδος] Jesus Christ, by whom he called us from darkness into light, from ignorance to full knowledge of his glorious name . . . etc [εἰς ἐπίγνωσιν δόξης ὀνόματος αὐτοῦ].[33]

In the context this sounds very like a reference to the gift of baptism. Both the significant words φῶς and ἐπίγνωσις occur here. The other quotation is from 2 Clement, which J. B. Lightfoot believed was a Christian homily delivered in Corinth some time between A.D. 120 and 140. Thus it is by no means outside our period. The final blessing runs (XX.5): "To the only God, invisible, Father of truth, who sent forth to us the Saviour and Prince of incorruptibility [ἀρχηγὸν τῆς ἀφθαρσίας], by whom he manifested to us the truth and the heavenly life, to him be glory for ever and ever. Amen."[34] It is possible that the phrase "he manifested to us the truth and the heavenly life" is a reference to the two sacraments, as well as being a general description of the Christian life. It seems to me quite possible that the author of 2 Clement inserts at the end of his work a quotation from his eucharistic prayer. In much the same way as the Epistle of Jude is lightened at the end by the lovely ascription, so the tone of this by no means exalted epistle is heightened by this ending. One may be permitted to conjecture that in both cases the author has enlivened exhortation by means of contemporary liturgy. Thus the notion of Christ "bringing to light" immortality, found in 2 Timothy 1.10, is not as strange as it seems. It is not intended to suggest that immortality was there all the time and only had to be disclosed. It is an indirect reference to baptism and perhaps to the eucharist.

It may therefore be reasonably claimed that we do have a direct reference to the eucharist in 1 Timothy 4.1–5, and probably a less direct one in 2 Timothy 1.10. The very fact that the author does not go out of his way to impart teaching about the eucharist, but uses the existence of the eucharist as an argument against his doctrinal opponents, is itself an indication of how much the eucharist was an accepted part of church life by the time that the Pastorals were written. We suggested in the last chapter that the author of the Pastorals used his baptismal tradition as material for his Epistle, adapting it for his purpose, much as (we claimed) the authors of Ephesians and 1 Peter respectively did. Much the same could be said of his eucharistic references in 1 and 2 Timothy, except that they are less extensive and the reference in 1 Timothy 4 is more of an illustration than a quotation, though the parallels from the Didache suggest that he does have some sort of a formula in mind.

But it would be a mistake to imagine that there was in the period of the writing of the Pastorals a clear-cut distinction between a baptismal prayer and a eucharistic prayer. Indeed one should not think in terms of prayer books and fixed offices: a baptism would also imply a eucharist and the prayer used at baptism would simply be an extension or adaptation of the eucharistic prayer. Thus, when we attempt to trace eucharistic references in the Pastorals we are not really doing anything very different from what we did when we found references to a baptismal liturgy. Indeed, once grant Boismard's thesis that we have elements of a baptismal liturgy in Titus, eucharistic references are very much what we should expect to find as well. Nor must we imagine that such references as we have to the eucharistic prayer are part of a fixed liturgy in our modern sense of the word. The author is utilizing his own eucharistic tradition; we may be sure that it was neither unalterably fixed nor entirely fluid. There were certain things that should be included, and the author gives us some idea of how he was accustomed to express some of them.

One last point should be made: the parallel we have drawn between 1 Timothy 4.1–5 and the Didache would suggest in itself that the eucharistic tradition with which the author of the Pastorals was acquainted was much the same as that which we find in the Didache, that is to say, that it associated the eucharist with communion, fellowship, and unity rather than with cross, death, and covenant. It has often been claimed by commentators on the Didache, not least by Lietzmann himself, that it represents a non-Pauline tradition of the eucharist.[35] But it can hardly be denied that the author of the Pastorals was acquainted with 1 Corinthians;[36] he must therefore have known of Paul's tradition. He professed to be (and no doubt believed himself to be) a disciple of Paul; he was attempting to preserve the tradition of Paul's teaching in the Church of his day. This reflection would suggest that at least the more extreme versions of Lietzmann's theory cannot hold water. Whatever may be said in defence of the theory that there were two traditions of the eucharist in the early Church, one stemming from Paul and one from the general practice of Jesus, they seem to be able to live together quite happily in the faith and practice of the author of the Pastorals. We may well agree with R. D. Richardson when he says: "The idea that St Paul perpetuated the remembrance of the Last Supper, while the first disciples passed it by to perpetuate the general Supper-practice of Jesus, is clearly the result of a logical reasoning that overrides the probabilities of the human situation."[37]

9

The Significance of the
Pastoral Epistles

One of the most puzzling features about the Pastoral Epistles is the impression they make when one reads them carefully and attentively. When one reads the undeniably Pauline Letters or Hebrews, one is carried along by the argument. It may be the case, as in 1 Corinthians, that the writer passes from one topic to another fairly frequently. But while he is dealing with his topic he gives the impression of concentrating on it; one is aware of a powerful mind behind the words, a unifying purpose. Quotations are part of the argument. There are few, if any, loose ends. Reading the Pastorals gives one a very different impression: one seems to be listening to a series of rather pedestrian remarks, varied by occasional flashes of quite different material, often introduced with no very great relevance to the topic in hand. There is a complete absence of unifying theme; one comes across sentences which are interesting and challenging in themselves, but do not seem very closely related to their context. To use a rather Victorian metaphor, Paul, or the author of Hebrews, is a broad, sweeping river, very deep in places and always in visible motion, plainly moving onwards to its destination. The Pastorals are a meandering brook, but a brook which contains unexpected pools of remarkable depth. It is this impression of relative incoherence which, as much as anything else, makes it impossible to believe that the great bulk of the Pastorals is Pauline.

This strange feature is, I believe, best accounted for by the supposition that the author of the Pastorals had no theology of his own. He is a purveyor of other men's theology. What he supplies is a fairly conventional piety and a strong moral earnestness. This is not to suggest that he was a mere magpie, one who collected any bits of liturgy or confession within his grasp and strung them together like beads on a string, quite unaware of their mutual incompatibility. There are, it is true, one or two places, where the theological principles implicit in his language are not strictly speaking consistent; in 2 Timothy 2.19–21, for example, I think he is uneasily combining a Johannine belief in the indefectibility of the elect with a Pauline conviction that it is quite possible to cease to be a member of the Church and even perhaps return to the fold later. And I have suggested that the mediator-Christology implicit in 1 Timothy 2.5 is not ultimately compatible with the consubstantiability of the Father with the Son, which I believe to be implicit in both Pauline and Johannine Christology. But these are inconsistencies which lie fairly deep down in a man's theology, and the author of the Pastorals is not to be accused of holding a merely muddled Christology, such as one finds, for instance, in the Shepherd of Hermas.

The true position seems to be that the author, while consciously adhering to as much of Paul's theology as he understood, also gives us evidence of other types of theology. This is particularly evident in his Christology, as far as we can recover it. For example, our study of that word *hedraiōma* in 1 Timothy 3.15 has shown that the Christology lying behind that whole verse is much closer to that of Acts 7 and Hebrews than to Paul. Indeed here the author is also nearer to the Johannine tradition, with its emphasis on Christ as the place where God is to be worshipped. Hans Windisch maintains in fact that we find in the Pastorals a primitive, pre-Pauline *anthrōpos*-Christology,[1] which was strictly incompatible with a *theos*-Christology. He sees complete subordination of Christ to the Father throughout, and he denies that there is in the Pastorals a belief in the pre-existence of Christ in any but a vague ideal sense. He thus has to translate τοῦ μεγάλου Θεοῦ καὶ σωτῆρος ἡμῶν Ἰησοῦ Χριστοῦ in Titus 2.13 as "of our great God and our Saviour Jesus Christ", which involves strange implications about the Parousia. He also finds the closest parallel to the Christology of the Pastorals in the early speeches in Acts, and thus reaches the paradoxical conclusion that it should be called a *pais Theou* Christology, even though Christ is never called *pais Theou* in the Pastorals. I believe that a study of the Old Testament passages used by the author of the Pastorals makes it very difficult to deny that he did believe in the full pre-existence of Christ, or at least his sources did. But Windisch's article is valuable in its emphasis on the non-Pauline elements in the author's Christology, and we can heartily endorse his sentiments when he writes: "He [the author of the Pastorals] has no theological Christology, but only teaching about Christ in the form of statements, formulae, and hymns, which spring from various orders of teaching and teaching material."

Nowhere, perhaps, is the author more different from Paul than in his treatment of the Old Testament. Except when he is deliberately copying Paul (as, for example, in 1 Timothy 5.17–18), he does not go direct to the Old Testament himself. When Paul needed a midrash on the Old Testament, he composed it himself, as in 1 Corinthians 10.1–11, or 2 Corinthians 3. The author of the Pastorals incorporates other people's midrash into his own material, as in 1 Timothy 3.15; 2 Timothy 2.19–21. The obvious exception to this would seem to be 1 Timothy 2.11–15, the passage on Eve's transgression. But here also he is following Paul; his own additions to the midrash are original, but we may conjecture that he treated the passages in Genesis only because his master Paul had already referred to them.

It is only fair to point out, however, that in thus purveying other people's theology the author is simply following his own declared principles. He repeatedly emphasizes throughout all three Epistles that Timothy and Titus are to guard carefully the sacred tradition and hand it on intact. As several editors have pointed out, the last thing that the author of Pastorals would have wanted to be was "an original theologian". His great objection to the teachers whom he condemns was that they were original, that is, they imported their own ideas into the authentic gospel. The author was not capable, as were Paul, John, and the author of Hebrews, of illuminating and extending the significance of Jesus Christ by his own presentation. He therefore did what was in the circumstances much more useful, he purveyed the interpretations of others in the form of hymn, prayer, confession, and midrash.

As we have noted in the introduction, those modern scholars who still defend the Pauline authorship of the entire Pastorals base their arguments very largely on the traces of Jewish influence and Jewish tradition which are to be found in them. It is quite true that there is much Jewish traditional belief and teaching to be found lying behind the Pastorals, and it would be a complete misunderstanding to maintain that the Pastorals represent a radical Hellenization of the Pauline gospel. But the trend of these studies has surely been to suggest that the author of the Pastorals was in contact with Hellenistic rather than with Palestinian Judaism, and that he did not have first-hand access to rabbinic tradition. There is, it seems to me, very little to suggest that he knew any Hebrew at all,[2] and at various important points he seems to belong to a distinctly more Hellenistic milieu than did Paul: consider, for example, our conclusions about his views on the inspiration of scripture which we reached in Chapter 4. Again, we must not forget the remarkable link with 1 Clement which we have observed at more than one point (see Table 1). This does not mean that either the author copies 1 Clement or that 1 Clement copied the author. But it does suggest a very similar milieu, and few would deny that Clement is writing from a more Greek and less Jewish milieu than Paul. We might bring in here also the question of awareness of Philo's writings. It seems to me difficult to avoid the conclusion that the author knew of some of Philo's writings. It is natural to suggest that the two works *Quaestiones in Genesim* and *Quaestiones in Exodum* would be the sort of literature that would have a special appeal to the author of the Pastorals. We must allow that Philo was known to the author of the Hebrews.[3] But there is no compelling reason to believe that Paul used Philo's works at all. He could have read them, as the two men were almost exact contemporaries, but there is no evidence that he did.[4] It may be that the tendency to defend the authenticity of the

Pastorals on the grounds of their Jewish character is really only part of a justified reaction against the view that the Church almost immediately lost virtually all contact with Judaism. Pastorals may look Jewish only because the whole New Testament is in fact more Jewish than had been often supposed in a previous generation. It is significant also that in such a work as Daniélou's *La Théologie du Judéo-Christianisme* there are relatively few references to the Pastorals, despite the fact that Daniélou takes the full Pauline authorship for granted. Those that are there mostly refer to Daniélou's very disputable treatment of the ministry in the Pastorals. Compare also W. H. Brownlee's judgement: "[The Pastoral Epistles] seem to show the least kinship with the Qumran Scrolls of the entire New Testament". He dismisses the idea that the New Testament *episcopoi* can be found in the "overseers" of the Qumran Community.[5]

In the scholarly debate about the origin of the ordained ministry which has been going on during the last seventy years (with particular emphasis in this country) much use has been made of the phrase "the tunnel period". This means the period between the Pauline Church and the universal emergence of the threefold ministry in the third or fourth decade of the second century. The debate has died down for the moment and it cannot be said that there has been any remarkable new discovery in the sphere of the ministry that has decided the matter one way or the other. But, if it could be generally accepted that the Pastoral Epistles belong to the very early years of the second century, then it could be claimed that, not in the sphere of the ministry but in that of worship, there is a good deal of light now to be found in the tunnel. Nearly every modern scholar, even those such as Jeremias who still defend the Pauline authorship of the Pastorals, agrees that there is liturgical material in the Pastorals. If these studies have any validity, then the Pastorals do contain a number of liturgical fragments, and we can form some notion of how the Christian Church was conducting its public worship, at least in Asia Minor, at the beginning of the second century.

First of all, there were baptismal formulas—I do not mean

formulas of administration, which are not given, but a baptismal prayer (incorporating an act of praise)[6] which was shared, at least in many features, among more than one church. Perhaps what we have is the baptismal prayer belonging to the tradition of the church in Asia Minor, or a part of Asia Minor. Then there was a long prayer, for use in regular public worship, a prayer which included intercessions and praise. We have claimed that Clement gives us an example of this prayer and that 1 Timothy 2.1–7 gives us something like an outline of it. We cannot be certain that what Clement is giving us is a eucharistic prayer, but the evidence of the Pastorals suggests that this is what the author has in mind when he gives directions for public prayer, since his quotations from prayers in certain parts of his work do imply the context of the eucharist. When we first compare 1 Clement with the Pastorals, and then the Pastorals with the Didache, we do seem to see something like an unbroken tradition of the long public prayer, though it may well have been a developing tradition. It is true that in the prayer which Clement gives us, and the outline which the author of the Pastorals provides in 1 Timothy 2.1–7, there are no explicit eucharistic references. But we shall not perhaps be working *disciplina arcani* too hard if we call it in to account for this. And Clement does write "each man of you, brothers, should give thanks to God [εὐχαριστείτω τῷ Θεῷ] in his own order maintaining a good conscience, not transgressing the fixed range of his sacred office [τὸν ὡρισμένον τῆς λειτουργίας αὐτοῦ κανόνα] in a decent manner".[7] Whatever this may suggest as to full congregational participation in worship, it does seem to imply a eucharist in which various sections of the congregation have various offices, a liturgy not merely a prayer-meeting. We might, very tentatively, express it thus: in 1 Clement in A.D. 96 we find a long public prayer, an ordained ministry (presbyters and deacons), and relatively fixed functions for the orders (including, of course, the laity). In the Pastorals (? A.D. 105) we find an outline for a prayer, various formulas including a reference to a eucharistic formula (1 Timothy 4.5), and a fixed ministry (bishops/presbyters and deacons). In the Didache (? A.D. 120–30) we find two (alternative, perhaps) eucharistic prayers (the latter including responses from the laity), and a local ministry consisting of bishops and deacons. This looks like a eucharistic tradition with the long eucharistic prayer as its back-bone.

Naturally, we have to make full allowance for the fact that it was not fixed in the way liturgies became fixed later. Clement no doubt gives the local Roman version of the eucharistic prayer, perhaps even his own particular version. The very fact that the author of the Pastorals gives directions about how public prayer is to be made shows that it was not taken for granted. The alternative prayers in the Didache (if they are alternatives) suggest plenty of latitude for individuals; and we must not forget that the prophets were probably free to pray in their own words.[8] But, with all these allowances, it can still be claimed that we have an outline of a eucharistic prayer during this period. The darkness is not complete, and the evidence of the Pastorals plays an essential part in our enlightenment.

C. K. Barrett remarks in his commentary on the Pastorals: "For the Pastorals do not show us 'Primitive Catholicism' (whether this be taken as a term of praise or opprobium), so much as developed Paulinism."[9] *Frühkatholismus* is a term which has been invented by German scholars, most of whom were Lutherans, and, unless defined very carefully, it carries with it the implication that catholicism was a sign of the degeneracy of the Church, a falling away from the high Pauline period when all was conducted on a lofty basis of justification by faith. This is, of course, absurd. But there is a certain sense in which one could say that *Frühkatholismus is* developed Paulinism. Presumably the essence of *Frühkatholismus* consists in the appearance of a fixed ordained ministry, of fixed forms of worship, and of authoritarian methods of ruling the Church such as excommunication for heresy. Perhaps a critic of *Frühkatholismus* would add a tendency towards legalism in ethics and a certain absorption of the *mores* of the Hellenistic world in which the Church was set. Now it cannot be denied that every one of these features is to be found in the Pastorals, as contrasted with the genuinely Pauline Epistles, in which they are either absent or else only rudimentary. But, with the exception of the last (pagan *mores*) it is difficult to see how the Church could have survived in the world without developing in this manner. The main reason why the ordained ministry is not prominent in Paul's writings is no doubt that he did not expect the Church to last long enough to need a very permanent structure of ministry. The experience of the Church in non-Christian environments in Asia and Africa during the last two centuries surely suggests that without a fairly strict discipline it cannot survive, but it is inevitably absorbed in its environment. And it is impossible to deal on a basis of grace and love alone with those who are determined to act on a purely legal basis; in other words, those who will not live by grace must live by law, an insight which is implicit in Paul's own gospel. What we find to some extent in the Pastorals is this insight being worked out in life: when members of the Christian Church refuse the life of grace and love and behave towards their fellow-Christians on a basis of legalism and power politics, the only way the Church can defend itself is by exercising discipline, which itself involves the application of law, not grace, and should be used only where the relationship of grace in love has broken down.

As for the emergence of fixed forms of worship, here surely we can reasonably maintain that we are clearly the gainers. We do not know very much about what forms of worship were used in Paul's day, but the evidence with which the author of the Pastorals provides us about liturgical usage in the Church of his day must impress us with the richness and the depth of the liturgical tradition which had already accumulated. Certainly the Church was borrowing from Hellenistic Judaism. But this was a most rich and fertile source. The baptismal source which Boismard has traced, and which we have detected also in Ephesians, includes some of the finest passages in 1 Peter. The language of 1 Timothy 3.15 may be puzzling, but it is not feeble or unimpressive. We may perhaps condemn Clement's long prayer for undue verbosity, but it is not the verbosity of an exhausted tradition, it is the exuberance of a new movement just gathering strength. Even the christological formulas which the author has presented, or the christological midrash which we have detected in his work, different though they may be from Paul's, are not necessarily inferior. On the contrary, the more we try to penetrate into the background of the author's church life, the more we are impressed by the richness and variety of what we find there. The author did not contribute very much to it himself, but he preserved it for us. As one studies the various ways in which the great writers of the New Testament present their theology, Paul, John, the author of Hebrews, one is always being brought back to the same thought: astonishing variety, but underlying unity of theme. They expressed themselves with great and original individuality, but they were writing about the same central thing. The same can be said, arrived at by a rather different method, about the Pastoral Epistles. The author gives us a glimpse into a great and developing variety, but the underlying unity is still there.[10]

So far in this work we have scrupulously avoided attempting to fix the date and provenance of the Pastoral Epistles. The aim has been to begin from the text, and to pursue certain lines of investigation which the text seemed to open up. But it would seem lacking in spirit not to attempt to draw from our studies some conclusions about the relation of the Pastorals to contemporary Christian literature, tentative though these conclusions must be. In the first place, it must be said that at every point these studies have reinforced the belief that the Pastoral Letters were not written by Paul, nor by a close disciple of Paul, but by someone who lived considerably later than Paul.[11] Next, I believe that the author evinces a knowledge of Romans, 1 and 2 Corinthians, and Philippians as Pauline Epistles. There are no signs in the text of the Pastorals that the author knew Colossians, but I find it very hard to believe that in fact he did not. This is because I believe that 2 Timothy 4.12 is a genuinely Pauline fragment, and that the letter of which this verse is a fragment was not sent to someone who was in Ephesus, but to one who was in a place fairly accessible to Ephesus. This place I believe to be Colossae, in view of 2 Timothy 4.10-12 with its reference to Demas and Luke and

Tychicus, also mentioned in Colossians 4.7–14.[12] If the author found a letter of Paul's, or part of it, at Colossae, it is impossible to believe that he did not know the Epistle to the Colossians. If he knew Colossians, he may well have known Philemon also. He shows no knowledge of Galatians or the Thessalonian Epistles. This does not necessarily imply that they did not form part of his Pauline Corpus. Acts he certainly knew (see 2 Timothy 3.10–11) and therefore very probably Luke also.

There is no evidence which compels us to believe that the author knew Ephesians as an Epistle. As we have noted, all the material which he has in common with Ephesians seems to come from his common baptismal tradition, which he also shares with 1 Peter. It seems to me, therefore, safer to suggest that he shared a common source tradition with these two Epistles rather than to claim that he knew them. The evidence would suggest that he was a fairly close contemporary with both of them. Of the Johannine Epistles it can also be said that there is some evidence that they shared certain elements in a common baptismal tradition, though the link is not nearly as close as with Ephesians and 1 Peter. Here too it seems to be matter of two contemporaries writing independently.[13]

To place the Pastorals, not merely chronologically, but in relation to the whole of relevant primitive Christian literature, is more difficult. But it is worth attempting. If one were to try to fix the position of the Pastorals in respect of their witness to, and significance for, the gospel, for apostolic Christianity, one would probably put them somewhere between 1 Peter and the Johannine Epistles on the one hand, and Ignatius, or 2 Peter, on the other. Perhaps the position could best be plotted on a diagram:

$$\uparrow$$

Paulines			Luke–Acts
Ephesians	Hebrews		Revelation
1 Peter		Johannine Epistles	
Clement		Pastoral Epistles	
	Ignatius		
Hermas	2 Peter	Jude	Barnabas	Didache

The arrow indicates the direction in which they point, that is towards the gospel, towards the series of events round which the New Testament is written. The lower down the page a work appears, the farther it is from the central theme. This is, of course, a value judgement. Others would say perhaps that the Pastorals should be put higher, and Clement lower. Still others would be shocked that 2 Peter should be placed so far from the centre. It cannot be denied that chronology is an element in forming the value judgement, but this is not a chronological scheme. We have been used recently to hear the New Testament spoken of as primarily a record. Here is one, subjective, attempt to set the Pastorals in their relation to that record.[14]

One might end with what sounds like a paradox: if we judge the Pastoral Epistles by the criterion of what they claim to be, we are bound to find them wanting. But if we judge them on the basis of what they are, we shall probably end by valuing them highly. If they are Pauline, they represent a dismal conclusion to Paul's writings; if they are post-Pauline, they are an admirable and indispensable illustration of the state of the Church at the end of the first century.

Notes

CHAPTER 1

[1] J. B. Phillips, *Letters to Young Churches* (14th impression, London 1959).

[2] *Expository Times*, Vol. VIII (July 1897), p. 471.

[3] C. Spicq, O.P., *Les Épîtres Pastorales* (Paris 1947).

[4] J. A. Montgomery and H. S. Gehman in the ICC on 1 Kings (Edinburgh 1951) suggest that ἐπὶ καινότητος represents *bachnukkāh* "at the festival of the dedication", and is therefore originally a rubric and not part of the text. But H. St J. Thackeray in an art. "New Light on the Book of Jashar" in *JTS*, Vol. XI (1910), pp. 518 f, explains τοῦ κατοικεῖν as a mistranslation of *leshābhāth* "for the sabbath" and ἐπὶ καινότητος as part of a musical direction.

5. Philo, *Opera Omnia*, ed. L. Cohn and P. Wendland, Vol II (Berlin 1897), p. 143.

[6] See D. Barthélemey, O.P., art. "Chainon Manquant de l'Historie de la Septante" in *RB*, Vol. 60 (1953), p. 18.

[7] *Biblia Sacra Vulgatae Editionis* (edn of Sixtus V and Clement VIII, London n.d.).

[8] H. von Soden, *Hand-Kommentar z. N.T. Die Pastoral Briefe* (old series, Freiburg 1891).

[9] Quoted in C. F. Burney, *Notes on the Hebrew Text of the Books of Kings* (Oxford 1903 in loc.).

[10] I have elaborated this point in my book *Jesus Christ in the Old Testament* (London 1965), pp. 10 f.

[11] Pp. 83 f.

[12] See R. P. C. Hanson, art. "Studies in Texts: Acts 6.13" in *Theology* Vol. LI (April 1947), p. 142.

[13] *The Beginnings of Christianity*, ed. F. J. Foakes-Jackson and Kirsopp Lake (London 1953).

[14] I have translated all quotations from Ps. 132 from the LXX, for it is perfectly clear that the author of Stephen's speech read his Old Testament Greek.

[15] Cohn and Wendland's edn, op. cit., Vol III (Berlin 1898).

[16] Cf. also ibid., 185, where Philo struggles hard to prove that in Gen. 28.16 when Jacob says, "Surely the Lord is in this place", he does not mean that God was in the place. But Philo's interest was different from Stephen's. Philo

was chiefly concerned to maintain that God was not in any *topos*, but every *topos* was in God.

[17] F. J. Foakes-Jackson, art. "Stephen's Speech" in *JBL*, Vol. XLIX (1930), p. 283.

[18] M. Simon, art. "Saint Stephen and the Jerusalem Temple" in the *Journal of Ecclesiastical History*, Vol. 2 (1951), p. 127.

[19] L. W. Barnard, art. "St Stephen and Alexandrian Christianity" in *NTS*, Vol. 7 (1960–1), pp. 31 f.

[20] The LXX has misread the Hebrew, which is "has set the sun in the heavens".

[21] J. B. Lightfoot, *The Apostolic Fathers* (London 1898), p. 262.

[22] O. Cullmann, art. "L'Opposition contre le Temple de Jerusalem, motif commune de la theologie Johannique et du Monde Ambiant" in *NTS*, Vol. 5 (1958–9), pp. 157 f.

[23] G. Wagner, art. "La Tabernacle et la Vie en Christ" in *RHPR*, Vol. 41 (1961), pp. 379 f.

[24] B. F. Westcott, *The Gospel according to St John* (London 1900).

[25] H. J. Holtzmann, *Hand-Commentar z, N.T., Evangelium, Briefe, und Offenbarung des Johannes, besorgt von W. Bauer* (Tübingen 1908).

[26] See R. H. Charles, *Apocrypha and Pseudepigrapha of the O.T.*, Vol. I, Sirach, ed. G. H. Box and W. O. E. Oesterley (Oxford 1913) in loc.

[27] F. Blass and A. Debrunner, *A Greek Grammar of the N.T., etc.*, Eng. tr. and ed. R. W. Funk (Cambridge and Chicago 1961).

[28] LXX λύχνος, MT *nēr*.

[29] E. C. Hoskyns, *The Fourth Gospel*, ed. F. N. Davey (London 1947).

[30] R. Bultmann, *Das Evangelium des Johannes* (Göttingen 1941), p. 199.

[31] R. H. Lightfoot, *St John's Gospel*, a Commentary (Oxford 1956).

[32] C. H. Dodd, *The Interpretation of the Fourth Gospel* (Cambridge 1960), p. 205. The rabbi was described as *nēr ᶜōlām* and *nēr Yisrāēl*.

[33] C. K. Barrett, *The Gospel according to St John* (London 1955).

[34] M.-J. Lagrange, *Évangile selon Saint Jean* (Paris 1948).

[35] J. H. Bernard, *The Gospel According to St John*, ICC (Edinburgh 1928).

[36] MT for "a lamp to burn automatically" is *nēr tāmīd*.

[37] The Hebrew for "lantern" is *nēr*.

[38] It is hardly necessary to say that the use of these names does not necessarily imply a belief that these individuals wrote the respective works attributed to them.

[39] There are traces in the rabbinic tradition of the belief that all Israelites were originally intended to be priests in some sense; cf. the Mekilta de-Rabbi Ishmael, ed. and tr. J. Z. Lauterbach (Philadelphia 1933), Vol. II, p. 205: "Hence, the sages said: 'The Israelites before they made the Golden Calf were eligible to eat of the holy things, but after they made the Golden Calf, the holy things were taken from them and given to the priests exclusively.' "

This may therefore constitute an obscure but nevertheless real link between John 5.35 and 1 Peter 2. 1–10.

[40] B. Gärtner, *The Temple and the Community in Qumran and the N.T.* (Cambridge 1965). It is significant that Daniélou includes the concept of the pre-existent sanctuary among the theological themes which he claims are peculiar to Jewish Christianity. See J. Daniélou, *Théologie du Judéo-Christianisme* (Paris 1957), p. 323.

[41] I have discussed this passage in detail in *Jesus Christ in the Old Testament*, pp. 48–57.

[42] *Offenbarung und Schriftforschung in der Qumransekte* (Tübingen 1960), pp. 159f.

[43] See Betz, op. cit., p. 60.

[44] B.T.: Tractate *Hagiga*, ed. I. Abrahams (London 1938), pp. 69–70.

[45] B.T.: Tractate *Berakoth*, ed. Maurice Simon (London 1948), p. 205.

[46] B.T.: Tractate *Rosh Hashanah*, ed. Maurice Simon (London 1938), p. 65.

Only when this book was in proof did I see J. Murphy-O'Connor's important article "La 'Vérité' chez Saint Paul et à Qumran" in RB 72(1965), pp. 29–76. In it he draws out the parallel between *hedraiōma, alētheias,* and *sōdh 'emeth* in the Qumran documents very fully, emphasizing the conclusion that *hedraiōma* must refer to Timothy himself. But much of the force of this interpretation is lost if for other reasons one rejects the Pauline authorship of the Pastorals. Murphy-O'Connor himself on p. 76 of his article seems to prefer a theory that the Pastorals were edited "under Paul's aegis". Despite its admirably full treatment of the Qumran evidence, I remain quite unconvinced by the article as far as its main contention is concerned.

CHAPTER 2

[1] The alternative reading ὁμολογοῦμεν ὡς is obviously inferior.

[2] A. R. C. Leaney, *The Pastoral Epistles*, Torch Comm. Series (London 1960).

[3] *Interpreter's Bible*, ed. Pastoral Epistles, F. D. Gealy (New York 1955).

[4] So R. B. Townshend, ed. 4 Maccabees in R. H. Charles' *Apocrypha and Pseudepigrapha*, etc. Vol. II, p. 653. Daniélou (*Théologie du Judéo-Christianisme*, p. 53) actually puts it in the time of Ignatius of Antioch.

[5] 4 Maccabees strikes the modern reader as somewhat too rhetorical, but it has found some modern admirers, for example, Rabbi Samuel Sandmel in his book *We Jews and Jesus* (London 1965), p. 126, where he calls it "an extraordinarily beautiful book".

[6] O. Michel, art. ὁμολογουμένως in *TWNT*, Vol. V, 213 (ed. R. Kittel, Stuttgart 1954).

[7] B. S. Easton has noted the frequency of *eusebeia* in 4 Maccabees, but has not drawn any conclusions (*The Pastoral Epistles*, London 1948, in loc).

Similarly R. Falconer has noted the occurrence of *homologoumenōs* in 4 Maccabees, but has not elaborated it (R. Falconer, *The Pastoral Epistles*, Oxford 1937, in loc). So also Spicq in his *Excursus* on *eusebeia*.

[8] W. Foerster, art. "Εὐσεβεία in den Pastoralbriefen" in *NTS*, Vol. 5 (1958–9), pp. 213 f.

[9] In loc. 1 Tim. 3.15.

[10] Compare also Letter to Aristeas 139, where God is designated τὸν μόνον Θεὸν καὶ δύνατον, *Letter to Aristeas*, ed. P. Wendland (Teubner Library, Leipzig 1910).

[11] But in 2.15 there is good support for φιλαρχίας as a v. l.

[12] φιλάργυρος is found in Luke 16.14 and 2 Tim. 3.2 and ἀφιλάργυρος in Heb. 13.5 and 1 Tim. 3.3.

[13] λογισμὸς μὲν δὴ τοίνυν ἐστὶν νοῦς μετὰ ὀρθοῦ λόγου προτιμῶν τὸν σοφίας βίον.

[14] 2 Macc. 4.6; 4.40; 14.5; 15.33.

[15] 3 Macc. 3.20.

[16] But the first corrector in Codex Sinaiticus and one minuscule MS. omits ἀνοίας here.

[17] They are the Greek uncial G, some Old Latin manuscripts, the Gothic version, and Ambrosiaster. They are not, of course, of sufficient weight to displace "Jambres". Did this rendering perhaps originate with a copyist who was in touch with Talmudic tradition?

[18] See *Menahoth*, p. 513, ed. E. Cashdan (London 1948) in the Babylonian Talmud.

[19] See H. Odeberg, art. 'Ιαννῆς καὶ 'Ιαμβρῆς in Vol. III of *TWZNT* (Stuttgart 1939).

[20] R. H. Charles, *Apocrypha and Pseudepigrapha*, etc. Vol. II; in his edition of the fragment it is numbered VII, 19. Gaster translates "with his evil device" as "in his cunning" (T. H. Gaster tr. and ed. *The Scriptures of the Dead Sea Sect*, London 1957) and D-C tr. "*in seinen blosen Planen*".

[21] J. A. F. Gregg, *The Wisdom of Solomon* (Cambridge 1909).

[22] J. Reider, *The Wisdom of Solomon* (New York 1957).

[23] J. Weber, ed. "La Livre de sa Sagesse" in *La Sainte Bible*, ed. L. Pirot and A. Clamer (Paris 1946).

[24] J. Fichtner *Weisheit Salomos* (Handbuch z. A.T., Tübingen 1938).

CHAPTER 3

[1] D-C considers that the Wisdom passage has certainly influenced 2 Timothy 2.19–21.

[2] I have suggested in *The Wrath of the Lamb* (London 1959), pp. 90 f, that σκεύη ὀργῆς could mean "instruments of wrath" just as much as 'objects of

wrath", and that Paul deliberately refrained from saying explicitly that God made the vessels of wrath for destruction.

[3] C. K. Barrett in *The Pastoral Epistles* (Oxford 1963) well points out that a man can cleanse himself from wrong associations and that therefore there cannot be any question of predestination.

[4] Editors are, however, much divided on the question whether baptism is implied here or not. The older commentators tend to dismiss the idea. Thus von Soden in *Hand-Kommentar N.T.* (Freiburg 1891) says "Der Geist ist das Siegel", which leaves no room for baptism; and T. K. Abbott, *Epistles to the Ephesians and Colossians*, ICC (Edinburgh 1909), thinks the reference would be too obscure. G. Fitzer thinks there is no direct reference to baptism in either of the passages in Ephesians (art. σφράγις in *TWNT*, Vol. VII, Stuttgart, 1964). But G. W. H. Lampe writes: "His use of the aorist indicates that this union and the logical consequences of participation in the Spirit are thought of as directly related to a particular moment in the experience of the believer . . . there can be no doubt that the decisive moment to which Paul refers is baptism" (*The Seal of the Spirit*, London, 2nd edn 1967, p. 62; see also pp. 4–5; 56–7; 61). M. Dibelius in *Handbuch z. N.T. An die Kolosser Epheser, An Philemon* (Tübingen 1953, rev. D. H. Greeven) is inclined to this view also: "Hier soll das Wort vielleicht die Taufe bezeichnen", and he refers to Schlier as confirming this view. The case for baptism seems particularly strong in view of 4.30. The appeal to the readers on the basis of something already done bears an unmistakable resemblance to the appeal in 1 Corinthians 6.11, where few will deny that baptism is indicated. Compare also the frequent use of σφράγις in the Shepherd of Hermas for baptism: *Sim.* 8.VI.3; 9.XVI.3; XVII.4; XXXI.1,4. (J. B. Lightfoot (ed.), *The Apostolic Fathers*, London 1926). Daniélou is very emphatic that σφράγις meant baptism in the Jewish-Christian tradition. The image, he says, comes from Judaism. See *Théologie du J-C*, p. 384.

[5] J. Jeremias, art. ἀκρογωνιαῖος in *TWNT* Vol. I (Stuttgart 1949). See also my discussion of "apostles and prophets" in *The Pioneer Ministry*, pp. 40 f (London 1961).

[6] R. J. McKelvey, art. "Christ the Cornerstone" in *NTS*, Vol. 8 (July 1962), pp. 352 ff.

[7] J. N. D. Kelly, *The Pastoral Epistles* in Black's N.T. Comms. (London 1963).

[8] J. H. Bernard, *The Pastoral Epistles* (Cambridge 1899).

[9] E. F. Brown, *The Pastoral Epistles*, Westminster Commentary (London 1917).

[10] E. F. Scott, *The Pastoral Epistles*, Moffatt Comms. (London 1936).

[11] This point is well made by G. Kretschmer in *Studien zur frühchristlichen Trinitätstheologie* (Tübingen 1956), p. 213, n. 7. He has no hesitation whatever in taking the seal as referring to baptism.

[12] Besides ἀπόστητε, we might suggest that ἀκαθάρτου μὴ ἅπτεσθω was echoed in "if anyone purifies himself from what is ignoble" in 2 Tim. 2.21.

[13] Martin Noth (ed. *Leviticus* E. tr. London 1965 of original German, Göttingen 1962) considers that the Name is "not mentioned here out of reverence", so the repugnance to mentioning the name is already operating.

[14] H. Bietenhard, art. ὀνομάζειν in *TWNT*, Vol. V (Stuttgart 1954).

[15] B. T. Tractate *Sanhedrin* I (ed. J. Schachter and H. Freedman, London 1935), p. 379.

[16] *The Targums of Onkelos and Jonathan Ben Uzziel on the Pentateuch*, ed. and tr. J. W. Etheridge (London 1865), pp. 222. ff.

[17] P. Wernberg-Møller (ed. and tr.), *The Manual of Discipline* (London 1957) p. 31.

[18] See Millar Burrows, *The Dead Sea Scrolls of St Mark's Monastery*, reproduction and transliteration (New Haven, U.S., 1951).

[19] Millar Burrows (ed. and tr.), *The Dead Sea Scrolls* (London 1956), p. 372.

[20] T. H. Gaster (ed. and tr.), *The Scriptures of the Dead Sea Sect* (London 1957), pp. 61–2.

[21] It is true that Gaster does not think that cursing God is implied here. He believes that the blank which occurs after *dābhār'ᵃsher lō* in vii. 1 originally contained the name of the official who is cursed. But this is not a view which has commended itself to others.

CHAPTER 4

[1] Following the RSV mg.; the RSV text reads: "All scripture is inspired by God and profitable . . ."

[2] W. Lock, *The Pastoral Epistles*, ICC (Edinburgh 1924).

[3] In loc. 2 Tim. 3.15.

[4] D. G. Schrenk, art. γραφή in *TWNT*, ed. G. Kittel (Stuttgart 1949), Vol.I, pp. 749 ff.

[5] D. Guthrie, *The Pastoral Epistles* (London 1957).

[6] Schrenk insists that it must mean "each passage of the scriptures" here.

[7] Marcus' tr. from the Armenian (Loeb edn, London 1953).

[8] E. Schweizer in *TWNT*, Vol. II, p. 452, art. θεόπνευστος, slightly inclines to Jeremias' view, in so far as he sees no evidence of any carefully marked out theory of inspiration here, or of any "guarantee" theory of infallibility.

[9] See E. G. Selwyn, *The First Epistle of St Peter* (London 1946), in loc.

[10] Tr. from Millar Burrows, *The Dead Sea Scrolls* (London 1956), pp. 367 f.

[11] See F. F. Bruce, *Biblical Exegesis in the Qumran Texts* (London 1960), p. 9.

[12] Otto Betz, *Offenbarung und Schriftforschung in der Qumransekte* (Tübingen 1960), p. 81. Betz refers to the Manual of Discipline 8.16 as I QS 8.16 and to the Damascus Document 2.12 as CD 2.12.

[13] Burrows, op. cit., p. 328.

[14] In a review in *JTS*, Vol. 46 (1946), p. 220.

¹⁵ For ἀπὸ Θεοῦ ἄνθρωποι there is a well-supported *v. l.*, ἅγιοι Θεοῦ, but on the whole ἀπὸ Θεοῦ ἄνθρωποι is more likely to be original as being more difficult.

¹⁶ C. Bigg, *I and II Peter*, ICC (Edinburgh 1901).

¹⁷ H. von Soden (ed.), *I and II Peter*, in Hand-Kommentar z. N.T., ed. H. J. Holtzmann (Freiburg 1891).

¹⁸ C. E. B. Cranfield, *I and II Peter and Jude*, Torch Comms. (London 1960).

¹⁹ S-B. in loc. quotes plenty of rabbinic testimony condemning the view that Moses alone, and not God, might be the author of a passage from the scriptures.

²⁰ See S. A. Naber, *Flavii Josephi Opera Omnia* (Leipzig 1888), Vol. I, my translation. Von Soden has noticed this reference. Cf. Targum of Onkelos: "In that hour, the Word of the Lord opened her mouth and fitted her to speak" (Etheridge, op. cit., p. 420).

²¹ See S-B in loc.

²² See *Sanhedrin* II (ed. H. Freedman) in B.T. pp. 717 ff.

²³ The same word in Greek.

²⁴ See D-C in loc.

²⁵ Dom. J. Dupont, *Gnosis* (Louvain and Paris 1960, 2nd edn) pp. 151–72.

CHAPTER 5

¹ In *Peake's Commentary on the Bible*, rev. and ed. Matthew Black and H. H. Rowley (London 1962), p. 1002.

² Philip Carrington, *The Early Christian Church*, Vol. I (Cambridge 1957), p. 267.

³ See *Jesus Christ in the Old Testament*, pp. 97–9. A. Oepke in art. μεσίτης (*TWNT*, Vol. IV, pp. 602 ff) agrees that the mention of a mediator here implies the inferiority of the Law.

⁴ Op. cit., p. 622.

⁵ Lock has anticipated Daniélou in referring to Testament of Dan, VI. 2.

⁶ D-C specifically denies that there is any connection with the LXX here.

⁷ RSV mg. "Would that there were an umpire between us!"

⁸ It is a great pity that in the other passage in Job where a mediator is mentioned the LXX is hopelessly astray. This is Job 33.23, where Elihu mentions the possibility that there might be for sinful man "an angel, a mediator, one of the thousand, to declare for man what is right for him". The Hebrew verb here is *līts* used in the Hiph'il. It is all the more unfortunate because this verb also occurs in Job 16.21, which is the other "arbitration" passage. But here also the LXX is completely different. In Genesis 42.23 the same word is translated ἑρμηνεύτης by the LXX, where it means simply one who interprets from Egyptian into Hebrew. In Isaiah 43.27, where it means "spokesman", LXX feebly renders "rulers".

[9] E. K. Simpson, *The Pastoral Epistles* (London 1954), in loc.

[10] G. Wohlenberg, *Die Pastoralbriefe* in *Komm. z. N.T.* ed. T. Zahn (Leipzig 1906).

[11] *The Greek New Testament*, ed. K. Aland, M. Black, B. M. Metzger, and A. Wikgren (New York and London 1966).

[12] Counting XXXIX. 3.9 as two citations, since he incapsulates Job 15.15 into a citation of Job 4.1b—5.5.

[13] J. B. Lightfoot, ed. *The Apostolic Fathers* (London 1891). Lightfoot's tr., p. 64.

[14] Lightfoot's tr. The LXX here is completely different from the MT. Clement shows no sign of knowing the MT.

[15] Cf., for example, II. 7 with Titus 3.1; XXIX. 1 with 1 Tim. 2.8; and LXI. 2 with 1 Tim. 1.17.

[16] Tractate *Baba Bathra*, ed. Maurice Simon, in B.T. (London 1935), p. 80.

[17] Cf. the well-known passage in *Quis rerum divinarum Heres* 205–6. The Logos, speaking to men, says, "I stood between the Lord and you . . . that is neither uncreated as God, nor created as you, but midway between the two extremes." It is significant that the quotation in Deut. 5.5 describes Moses.

[18] J. H. Moulton and G. Milligan, *Vocabulary of the Greek Testament* (London 1930), sub. art.

[19] O. Cullmann, *The Earliest Christian Confessions* (E.T. London 1949) p. 42.

[20] O. Cullmann, op. cit., p. 45.

[21] That there is some connection between 1 Tim. 2.5–6 and 1 Clement LIX—LXI has already been noted by A. Strobel in an unpublished doctoral thesis "Schriftverständnis und Obrigkeitsdenken in der Ältesten Kirche" (Erlangen 1956), p. 14, and by O. Knoch in *Eigenart und Bedeutung der Eschatologie im theologischen Anfriss der ersten Clemensbrief* (Bonn 1964), p. 62. But neither of these writers examines it in detail.

[22] W. C. van Unnik argues that the prayer was intended for use in a prayer meeting, more of an eschatological than of a eucharistic nature. See art. "I Clement 34 and the Sanctus" in *Vigiliae Christianae*, Vol. V (1951), pp. 204 ff. But this conclusion is questioned by O. Knoch (op. cit., pp. 59–60). He would find definite eucharistic references in XXXVI. 2 and XLIV. 4.

[23] I should not at all wish to suggest that it does not, in some form, go back to Jesus himself. But we are not concerned with that question here.

[24] It would be very interesting if the Dead Sea Scrolls could throw light on the question of a mediator. Unfortunately, the light they afford is very fitful indeed. P. Wernberg-Møller (op. cit.) finds a reference to intercessors in the phrase 'ōchᵃzē 'ābūth of I QS ii 9, but no other scholar has accepted this interpretation, and the translations offered differ so widely in meaning that it would be very rash to draw any conclusions about it. More promising is I QH vi 13, where we have the phrase wᵃ'ēn mēlīts. Gaster translates this

(op. cit., p. 156): "There stands no intermediary among them", but he has to change *bānīm* by conjecture into *bēynam* in order to get this sense. *Mēlīts* is the same word as is used with the meaning "intercessor, mediator" in Job 16.20; 33.23. But, if Gaster's translation is correct, this passage, far from witnessing to belief in an intercessor among the Qumran sect, denies the need for one, since the members are already in the presence of God. (For the Hebrew text of the Hymns see E. L. Sukenik, *The Dead Sea Scrolls of the Hebrew University*, Jerusalem 1955.)

CHAPTER 6

[1] Following the mg. reading. The RSV text has "if she continues".

[2] Wm. Nauck, "Der Herkunft des Verfassers der Pastoralbriefe" (dissertation for Göttingen University 1950, unpublished), pp. 97 ff.

[3] P. Wendland (ed.), *Aristeae ad Philocratem Epistula* (Teubner Lib., Leipzig 1910), 250. The Greek is μετάπιπτον εὐκόπως διὰ παραλογισμοῦ, my. tr.

[4] Questions on Genesis I. 33, tr. Marcus.

[5] R. B. Townshend (ed.), 4 Maccabees in R. H. Charles, op. cit., Vol. II, his tr. This passage is referred to by P. W. Schmiedel, see below.

[6] Op. cit., p. 654.

[7] F. L. Cross (ed.), *The Oxford Dictionary of the Christian Church* sub. art. "Maccabees, the Book of".

[8] Questions on Genesis I. 47, tr. Marcus.

[9] *Legum Allegoriae* III. 59 ff.

[10] My tr. in each case. The Greek is πᾶσα οὖν ἀπάτη οἰκειοτάτη ἡδονῇ, δόσις δὲ αἰσθήσει and παρὰ τὴν τῆς ὀφιωδοῦς καὶ ποικίλης ἡδονῆς. Townshend refers to this passage.

[11] L. S. E. Wells (ed.), "The Books of Adam and Eve" in Charles, op. cit., Vol. II.

[12] Wells, op. cit., p. 126.

[13] So A. Plummer (ed.), *II Corinthians*, ICC (Edinburgh 1915).

[14] P. W. Schmiedel (ed.), *II Corinthians* in *Hand-Commentar z. N.T.* (Freiburg 1891), Vol. II.

[15] R. H. Strachan (ed.), *II Corinthians*, Moffatt Comms. (London 1935). D-C also supports the idea that Paul means seduction, in loc. 2 Timothy 2.13-15.

[16] E-B Allo (ed.), *II Corinthians* (Paris 1956).

[17] Jean Héring (ed.), *II Corinthians* (Neuchâtel and Paris 1958).

[18] A point strangely missed by A. Oepke in his art. ἀπατάω in *TWNT*, Vol. I, p. 383.

[19] In loc. 1 Timothy 2.13-15.

[20] Noted by Joh. Schneider in art. παράβασις in *TWNT*, Vol. V, p. 735.

[21] Grimm-Thayer, *A Greek-English Lexicon of the N.T.*, (4th edn, Edinburgh 1901), sub art.

[22] One MS. omits γῆ which may well have been a gloss. Theodotion (or his source) has presumably translated *baᶜᵃbhūrekhā* "for your sake" as if it came from *ᶜābhar* "pass over", and has used a literal equivalent from παραβαίνω "go over or aside".

[23] The romantic alternative "she shall be saved through the Childbearing [of Mary]" can hardly be entertained.

[24] See M. R. James, *The Apocryphal New Testament* (Oxford 1924), p. 34, his tr.

[25] James, op. cit., p. 38.

[26] H. St J. Thackeray, *The Relation of St Paul to Contemporary Jewish Thought* (London 1900), pp. 50–1.

[27] *Sanhedrin*, p. 178 in B. T. *Sanhedrin*, ed. J. Schachter and H. Freedman (London 1935).

[28] See *Pesahim*, p. 606, ed. H. Freedman in B.T. (London 1938).

[29] See *Sotah*, p. 61, ed. A. Cohen in B.T. (London 1936).

[30] But it is not likely that Paul knew it in the version in which it has survived, for the account of the original sin there is by no means the same as Paul's.

[31] Sir Robert Falconer makes this point clearly in an art. "I Timothy 2.14–15, Interpretative Notes" in *JBL* (1941), Vol. 60, p. 375.

[32] It is not certain whether this can be said of The Book of the Secrets of Enoch or not. Charles says that a part of it must have been originally written in Greek, but that other parts may have a Hebrew original. It is not possible, he adds, to distinguish which parts may go back to an original Hebrew.

[33] It would be possible to quote the Qumran sectaries as disagreeing with the view of Adam presented by the author of the Pastorals. I QS iv 23 is rendered by Wernberg-Møller (op. cit.) thus: "theirs (the upright) is all the glory of Adam, without deceit." His regular translation for *ᶜūlāh* in the Hebrew is "deceit". If this is correct, it would imply that, in the view of the Qumran sectaries, Adam was deceived.

CHAPTER 7

[1] F. L. Cross, *I Peter, A Paschal Liturgy* (London 1954).

[2] C. F. D. Moule, art. "The Nature and Purpose of I Peter" in *NTS*, Vol. 13 (1956–7), p. 1.

[3] A. R. C. Leaney, art. "I Peter and the Passover" in *NTS*, Vol. 10 (1963–4), pp. 238 ff.

[4] M.-E. Boismard, art. "Une Liturgie Baptismale dans la Prima Petri" in *RB*, Vol. 63 of 1956–7, pp. 182 ff and Vol. 64 of 1957, pp. 161 ff.

[5] T. C. G. Thornton, art. "I Peter, A Paschal Liturgy?" in *JTS*, Vol. 12 (NS) (1961), pp. 14 ff.

[6] Floyd V. Filson, art. "How much of the New Testament is Poetry?" in *JBL*, Vol. 67 (1948), p. 125.

[7] Compare also the conclusion reached by R. P. C. Hanson in *Tradition in the Early Church* (London 1962), pp. 59–68. He emphasizes that one cannot find "early credal formulae" in the New Testament.

[8] Cross, op. cit., p. 36.

[9] The Greek is as follows; Titus 2.14 ζηλωτὴν καλῶν ἔργων, 1 Peter 3.13 ἐαν τοῦ ἀγαθοῦ ζηλωταὶ γένησθε.

[10] See above, pp. 47 f.

[11] Philip Carrington, *The Primitive Christian Catechism* (Cambridge 1940), pp. 19 ff.

[12] K. Weidinger, *Die Haustafeln, ein Stück urchristlichen Paränese* (Leipzig (1928).

[13] Op. cit., p. 53.

[14] E. G. Selwyn, op. cit., p. 391.

[15] Op. cit., pp. 423 and 431.

[16] Compare also 1 Peter 2.1 with Titus 3.3, where φθόνος is common to both. There is a more extended reference to former pagan behaviour in 1 Peter 4.3–4, but many scholars doubt whether this is part of the baptismal document.

[17] Compare also Titus 3.2 with 1 Peter 3.15–16; they have the significant word πραΰτης in common.

[18] W. Lock, op. cit., p. xxiv.

[19] It would be out of place in the text to speculate about the authorship of 1 Peter. There is much to be said for W. Bornemann's theory, to be found in *ZNTW*, Vol. 19 (1919–20), pp. 143 ff, that, at least as far as 3.12, it is a baptismal address given by Silvanus in Asia Minor about A.D. 90. The other churches in Asia Minor heard about it, he suggests, and wanted copies, so it was sent to them. Long after, when apostolic documents were being collected, it was found. Silvanus was not a well-known figure; Peter was known to have witnessed the sufferings of Christ, so it was attributed to him. For the evidence to suggest that the author of 1 Peter was acquainted with Ephesians, see C. L. Mitton, art. "The Relationship between 1 Peter and Ephesians" in *JTS*, Vol. I (NS) (1950), pp. 67–73.

[20] T. C. G. Thornton, op. cit., p. 21.

[21] C. H. Dodd (ed.), *The Johannine Epistles*, Moffatt Comms. (London 1946) in loc.

[22] Oscar Cullmann, *Baptism in the New Testament* (E.T. London 1950), p. 15.

[23] Except that it recurs in this Epistle, 1 John 4.10.

[24] Leon Morris, art. "The Use of ἱλάσκεσθαι etc. in Biblical Greek" in *ET*, Vol. 62 (May 1951), pp. 227–33.

[25] A further argument against Leon Morris' rendering might be found in 1 John 4.10, where we should have to understand that the Father sent his Son in order to propitiate himself, a very difficult concept.

[26] F. L. Cross, op. cit., p. 34.

[27] Compare 1 Clement LIX. 2: "He has called us from darkness to light, from ignorance to the full knowledge of his glorious name", which I believe is very likely to be a reference to baptism.

[28] This is not incompatible with the suggestion that John read it as λόγος. I do not suggest that John is using the A-B tradition; only that he had Psalm 130 in mind, from which that tradition itself may be derived, in part at least.

CHAPTER 8

[1] F. E. Vokes, *The Riddle of the Didache* (London 1938).

[2] Vokes, op. cit., p. 220.

[3] See J. P. Audet, *La Didache* (Paris 1958). For a useful criticism of his thesis see R. P. C. Hanson, *Tradition in the Early Church*, pp. 173-4. Daniélou would agree with Audet that it contains material which goes back before A.D. 70. See *Théologie du Judéo-Christianisme*, pp. 38 ff. See also an interesting art. by H. J. Gibbins in *JTS*, Vol. 35 (1935), pp. 373 ff—"The Problem of the Liturgical Section of the Didache". He maintains that the prayers in chapters 9 and 10 are undoubtedly eucharistic and are much earlier than the setting in which they are placed. He would trace them back to the earliest Christian community in Judea. Alfred Adam brings evidence from Syriac sources to suggest that the Didache was a manual for the newly founded missionary churches in eastern Syria. He believes it was composed in Pella between A.D. 90 and 100. (See A. Adam, art. "Erwägungen zur Herkunft der Didache" in *Zeitschrift für Kirchengeschichte*, Vol. LXVIII (1957), pp. 1-47.)

[4] B. C. Butler, art. "The Two Ways in the Didache," *JTS*, Vol. 12 (1961), p. 27.

[5] B. Altaner, *Patrologie* (Freiburg 1951), p. 38.

[6] R. Glover, art. "The Didache's Quotations and the Synoptic Gospels" in *NTS*, Vol. 5 (October 1958), p. 12.

[7] *The Teaching of the Twelve Apostles*, ed. H. de Romestin (2nd edn, Oxford 1885), my translation.

[8] H. Leitzmann, *Messe und Herrenmahl* (3rd edn, Berlin 1935), E.T. by D. Reeve, *Mass and Lord's Supper* (London 1953) pp. 190 ff.

[9] Paul Drews, art. "Untersuchungen zur Didache" in *ZNTW*, Vol. 5 (1904), pp. 53 ff.

[10] Vokes, op. cit., p. 197. It may be in order here to say briefly why his view of the Didache as a work of the second half of the second century has not been accepted in this work. It depends on the assumption that, in order to give an appearance of antiquity, the author of the Didache has deliberately assigned to apostles an inferior position. This seems to me most unlikely. We can have some idea of how a post-apostolic generation looked on the apostles: probably in Ephesians, and certainly in 2 Peter, they are treated as

holy apostles, hieratic figures already assuming some of the characteristics of the images in the stained glass window. That many years later than either of these works they could have been deliberately underrated seems incredible. Similarly, Vokes suggests that the suppression of the presbyters and the reference to bishops and deacons together are further signs of a tendency to imitate New Testament language. But only once in the New Testament (Phil. 1.1) do bishops and deacons appear together formally, and, though only bishops and deacons are mentioned in 1 Timothy 3, the author of the Didache is acquainted with other parts of the Pastorals as well in which presbyters are mentioned.

[11] See Erik Peterson, art. cit., for the significance of the reference to the mountains; Harald Riesenfeld emphasizes the eschatological significance in an art. "Das Brot von den Bergen" in *Eranos*, Vol. 54 (1957), p. 142–50; this is in opposition to C. F. D. Moule in an art. in *JTS*, Vol. 6 (NS) (1955), pp. 240 ff "A Note on Didache 9.5" in which he stresses the parallel with John 6.

[12] R. D. Richardson, *A Further Enquiry into Eucharistic Origins etc.* (London 1958, fasc. 1–6), p. 270.

[13] As does, for example, H. J. Holtzmann in an art. "Das Abendmahl in Urchristentum", in *ZNTW*, Vol. 5 (1904), pp. 89 ff. Equally unconvincing is M. Dibelius' contention that the prayers are merely Christianized versions of table prayers belonging to Hellenistic Judaism, put forward in an art. "Die Mahl-Gebete der Didache" in *ZNTW*, Vol. 37 (1938), pp. 32 ff.

[14] Gregory Dix supports Vokes in his view that we have an agapē in chapters 9–10, but for very different reasons; see *The Shape of the Liturgy* (London 1945), pp. 90–2.

[15] Pierre Batiffol, art. "L'Eucharistie dans La Didache" in *RB*, Vol. 2 (1905), pp. 58 ff. See also J. Marty, art. "Étude des textes cultuels de prière conservés par les pères apostoliques" in *RHPR*, Vol. 10 (1930), pp. 90 ff.

[16] R. M. Woolley, *The Liturgy of the Primitive Church* (Cambridge 1910), p. 489.

[17] Since the Didache shows no sign of knowing the eucharistic tradition of the Pauline churches, we cannot use the disturbances censured in 1 Cor. 11.17–22 as evidence that agapē and eucharist must have been separated by the time the Didache was composed.

[18] O. Cullmann, *Early Christian Worship* (E.T., London 1953), pp. 20 ff.

[19] He does speak of "ein cultisches Motiv" and gives a cross-reference to Didache 10.

[20] G. A. Michell, *Eucharistic Consecration in the Primitive Church* (London 1948).

[21] Michell, op. cit., p. 5.

[22] J. G. Davies, *A Select Liturgical Lexicon* (London 1964) sub. art. "Consecration".

[23] A. W. F. Blunt (ed.), *Justin's Apology* (Cambridge 1911), my translation.

[24] προσφέρομαι cannot mean "offer" so this is not a reference to the sacrifice of the eucharist.

[25] One suggestion of W. Lock.

[26] As B. S. Easton suggests.

[27] This is J. N. D. Kelly's solution.

[28] E. J. Goodspeed, *Die Ältesten Apologeten* (Göttingen 1914), my translation.

[29] The Didache also applies this quotation to the Eucharist in 14.3.

[30] I have taken the translation of this passage from R. P. C. Hanson's rendering in *Justin Martyr's Dialogue with Trypho* (World Christian Books, London 1963), p. 69.

[31] Lightfoot, *Apostolic Fathers*, "The Shepherd of Hermas", my translation.

[32] "Ignatius' Epistles" in J. B. Lightfoot (ed.), *The Apostolic Fathers* (London 1926 edn), my translation.

[33] J. B. Lightfoot, op. cit. "1 Clement", my translation.

[34] See J. B. Lightfoot, op. cit. "2 Clement", my translation. Altaner thinks it very likely to belong to a period before 150 (op. cit., p. 76).

[35] See H. Lietzmann, op. cit., p. 193 of E.T.: "[in the Didache] there is no question of a memorial of the death of Jesus, of his body and the blood of the covenant, or of a remembrance of the Last Supper on the night of his betrayal. Thus we have here a type of the Lord's Supper with no reference to Mark or Paul."

[36] See W. Lock, op. cit., p. xxiv, for references.

[37] R. D. Richardson, op. cit., p. 273.

CHAPTER 9

[1] H. Windisch, art. "Zur Christologie der Pastoralbriefe" in *ZNTW*, Vol. 34 (1935), pp. 213 ff.

[2] The arguments of Wm. Nauck (op. cit., pp. 17, 22, 32, 61) seem to me quite unconvincing.

[3] Spicq has surely demonstrated this in his Commentary on Hebrews; but if proof positive were needed, surely it must be admitted that Hebrews 6.13–14 is inspired by *Legum. Alleg.* III.203.

[4] It is interesting to observe that P. N. Harrison concludes that the author has read some of Philo's works whereas Paul has not. See his art. "The Authorship of the Pastoral Epistles", in *ET*, Vol. 57 (1955–6), pp. 77 ff.

[5] W. H. Brownlee, *The Meaning of the Qumran Scrolls for the Bible* (New York and Oxford 1964), p. 150 n.

[6] In Clement's prayer it is noteworthy that praise of God is worked quite naturally into what is formally an intercession; see 1 Clement LIX. 3; LX. 1.

[7] 1 Clement XLI. 1 my translation.

[8] See Didache 10.7; this is the view of J. Marty, art. cit. in *RHPR*, Vol. 10 (1930), pp. 90 ff.

[9] C. K. Barrett, op. cit., p. 32.

[10] The whole question of *Frühkatholismus* has recently been very adequately

discussed from the Roman Catholic point of view by Karl Hermann Schelkle in *Wort und Schrift* (Düsseldorf 1966), pp. 117 ff.

[11] This does not imply that there are no genuinely Pauline fragments. I believe that, in fact, there are. I would define them as 2 Timothy 1.15–18; 4.9–21 (omitting v. 18); Titus 3.12–14.

[12] I have set out my reasons more fully in my edition of the Pastorals in the Cambridge Bible Commentary (Cambridge 1966), pp. 10 ff.

[13] See also P. Galtier, art. "La Reconciliation des Pécheurs dans la Première Épitre à Timothée" in *RSR*, Vol. 39 (1951), pp. 317 ff., where he suggests an interesting link between 1 Timothy 5.22 and 2 John 11.

[14] I have omitted Matthew, Mark, John, and James, because they do not seem to me to come within the orbit of the Pastorals.

Bibliography

BOOKS REFERRED TO IN THE TEXT

Abbott, T. K., *Epistles to the Ephesians and the Colossians* (Edinburgh 1909)

Allo, E. B., *Seconde Épitre aux Corinthiens* (Paris 1956)

Altaner, B., *Patrologie* (Freiburg 1951)

Barrett, C. K., *The Gospel according to St John* (London 1955)

—— *The Pastoral Epistles* (Oxford 1963)

Bernard, J. H., *The Pastoral Epistles* (Cambridge 1899)

—— *The Gospel according to St John* (Edinburgh 1928)

Betz, O., *Offenbach und Schriftforschung in der Qumransekte* (Tübingen 1960)

Bigg, C., *I and II Peter* (Edinburgh 1901)

Billerbeck, P., See Strack, H. L.

Black, M., ed. *Peake's Commentary on the Bible* with H. H. Rowley (London 1962)

Blass, F., and Debrunner, A., *A Greek Grammar of the New Testament etc.*, tr. and ed. F. W. Funk (Cambridge and Chicago 1961)

Blunt, A. W. F., *Justin's Apology* (Cambridge 1911)

Brown, E. F., *The Pastoral Epistles* (London 1917)

Brownlee, W. H., *The Meaning of the Qumran Scrolls for the Bible* (New York and Oxford 1964)

Bruce, F. F., *Biblical Exegesis in the Qumran Texts* (London 1960)

Bultmann, R., *Das Evangelium des Johannes* (Göttingen 1941)

Burney, C. F., *Notes on the Hebrew Text of the Books of Kings* (Oxford 1903)

Burrows, M., *The Dead Sea Scrolls* (London 1956)

Carrington, P., *The Primitive Christian Catechism* (Cambridge 1940)

—— *The Early Christian Church* (Cambridge 1957)

Charles, R. H., *Apocrypha and Pseudepigrapha of the Old Testament* (Oxford 1913)

Cohn, L., *Philo, Opera Omnia*, with P. Wendland (Berlin 1897 +)

K

Conzelmann, H., ed. 3rd edn of M. Dibelius, *Die Pastoralbriefe* (Tübingen 1955)

• Cranfield, C. E. B., *I and II Peter and Jude* (London 1960)

Cross, F. L., *I Peter, a Paschal Liturgy* (London 1954)

—— ed. *The Oxford Dictionary of the Christian Church* (Oxford 1957)

Cullmann, O., *The Earliest Christian Confessions*, E. tr. (London 1949)

—— *Baptism in the New Testament* E. tr. (London 1950)

Daniélou, J., *Théologie du Judéo-Christianisme* (Paris 1957)

Davies, J. G., *A Select Liturgical Lexicon* (London 1964)

Debrunner, A., See Blass, F.

De Romestin, H., *The Teaching of the Twelve Apostles* (Oxford 1885)

Dibelius, M., See Conzelmann, H.

—— *An die Colosser, Epheser, an Philemon*, ed. D. H. Greeven (Tübingen 1953)

• Dix, G., *The Shape of the Liturgy* (London 1945)

Dodd, C. H., *The Johannine Epistles* (London 1946)

—— *The Interpretation of the Fourth Gospel* (Cambridge 1960)

Dupont, J., *Gnosis*, 2nd edn (Louvain and Paris 1960)

Easton, B. S., *The Pastoral Epistles* (London 1948)

Epstein, I., *The Babylonian Talmud* (London 1935 +)

Etheridge, J. W., *The Targums of Onkelos and Jonathan ben Uzziel on the Pentateuch* tr. and ed. (London 1865)

Falconer, R., *The Pastoral Epistles* (Oxford 1937)

Fichtner, J., *Weisheit Salomos* (Tübingen 1938)

Foakes-Jackson, F. J., and Lake, Kirsopp, *The Beginnings of Christianity* (London 1920–33)

Gärtner, B., *The Temple and the Community in Qumran and the New Testament* (Cambridge 1965)

Gaster, T. H., *The Scriptures of the Dead Sea Sect* (London 1957)

Gealy, F. D., *The Pastoral Epistles*, Interpreter's Bible (New York 1955)

Gehmann, H. S., and Montgomery, J. A., *1 Kings* (Edinburgh 1951)

Gregg, J. A. F., *The Wisdom of Solomon* (Cambridge 1909)

Guthrie, D., *The Pastoral Epistles* (London 1957)

Hanson, A. T., *The Wrath of the Lamb* (London 1959)

—— *The Pioneer Ministry* (London 1961)

—— *Jesus Christ in the Old Testament* (London 1965)

—— *The Pastoral Letters* (Cambridge 1966)

Hanson, R. P. C., *Tradition in the Early Church* (London 1962)

Harrison, P. N., *The Problem of the Pastoral Epistles* (London 1921)

Héring, J., *La Deuxième Épitre aux Corinthiens* (Neuchâtel and Paris 1958)

Holtzmann, H. J., *Briefe und Offenbarung des Johannes*, ed. W. Bauer (Tübingen 1908)

Hoskyns, E., *The Fourth Gospel*, ed. F. N. Davey (London 1940)

James, M. R., *The Apocryphal New Testament* (Oxford 1924)

Jeremias, J., *Die Briefe an Timotheus und Titus* (Göttingen 1963 edn)

Kelly, J. N. D., *The Pastoral Epistles* (London 1963)

Kittel, R., ed. *Theologisches Wörterbuch zum Neuen Testament* (Stuttgart 1954)

Knoch, O, *Eigenart und Bedeutung der Eschatologie im theologischen Aufris der ersten Clemensbrief* (Bonn 1964)

Kretschmer, G., *Studien zur frühchristlichen Trinitätstheologie* (Tübingen 1956)

Lagrange, M. J., *Évangile selon Saint Jean* (Paris 1948)

Lake, Kirsopp. See Foakes-Jackson, F. J.

Lampe, G. W. H., *The Seal of the Spirit* (London 1951)

Lauterbach, J. Z., ed. and tr. *The Mekilta de-Rabbi Ishmael* (Philadelphia 1933)

Leaney, A. R. C., *The Pastoral Epistles* (London 1960)

Lietzmann, H., *Messe und Herrenmahl* (Berlin 1935, 3rd edn), E. tr. by Dr Reeve, *Mass and Lord's Supper* (London 1953)

Lightfoot, J. B., *The Apostolic Fathers* (London 1895)

Lock, W., *The Pastoral Epistles* (Edinburgh 1924)

Marcus, R., ed. and tr. *Philo's Questions on Genesis* and *Questions on Exodus* (Loeb edn, London 1953)

Michell, G. A., *Eucharistic Consecration in the Early Church* (London 1948)

Milligan, G., and Moulton, J. H., *Vocabulary of the Greek New Testament* (London 1930 edn)

Montgomery, J. A., See Gehmann, H. S.

Moulton, J. H., See Milligan, G.

Naber, S. A., *Flavius Josephus, Opera Omnia* (Leipzig 1888)

Nauck, W., *Der Herkunft des Verfassers der Pastoralbriefe*, Diss. (Göttingen 1960)

Noth, M., *Leviticus*, E. tr. of German 1952 edn (Göttingen 1962)

Phillips, J. B., *Letters to Young Churches* (London 1959)

Plummer, A., *II Corinthians* (Edinburgh 1915)

Reider, J., *The Wisdom of Solomon* (New York 1957)

Richardson, R. D., *A Further Enquiry into Eucharistic Origins etc.* (London 1958)

Rowley, H. H., See Black, M.

Sandmel, S., *We Jews and Jesus* (London 1965)

Schelkle, K. H., *Wort und Schrift* (Düsseldorf 1966)

Schmiedel, P. W., *Der Zweite Brief an die Korinther* (Freiburg 1891)

Scott, E. F., *The Pastoral Epistles* (London 1936)

Selwyn, E. G., *The First Epistle of St. Peter* (London 1946)

Simpson, E. K., *The Pastoral Epistles* (London 1954)

Spicq, C., *Les Épitres Pastorales* (Paris 1947)

Strachan, R. H., *II Corinthians* (London 1935)

Strack, H. L., and Billerbeck, P., *Kommentar z. Neuen Testament etc.* (3rd edn, Munich 1961)

Strobel, A., *Schriftverständnis und Obrigkeitsdenken in der Ältesten Kirche,* Diss. (Erlangen 1956)

Sukenik, E. L., *The Dead Sea Scrolls of the Hebrew University* (Jerusalem 1955)

Thackeray, H. St. J., *The Relation of St. Paul to Contemporary Jewish Thought* (London 1900)

Thayer, J. H., ed. *Grimm's Greek-English Lexicon* (Edinburgh 1901, 4th edn)

Vokes, F. E., *The Riddle of the Didache* (London 1938)

Von Soden, H., *Die Pastoral Briefe* (Freiburg 1891)

—— *Die Briefe Petri* (Freiburg 1891)

Weber, J., *Le Livre de la Sagesse* in *La Sainte Bible*, ed. L. Pirot and A. Clamer (Paris 1946)

Weidinger, K., *Die Haustafeln, ein Stück urchristlichen Paränese* (Leipzig 1928)

Wendland, P. See Cohn, L.

Wernberg-Møller, P., *The Manual of Discipline* (London 1957)

Westcott, B. F., *The Gospel according to St John* (London 1900)

Wohlenberg, G., *Die Pastoralbriefe* (Leipzig 1906)

Woolley, R. M., *The Liturgy of the Primitive Church* (Cambridge 1910)

ARTICLES REFERRED TO IN THE TEXT

Adam, A., "Erwägungen zur Herkunft der Didache" in *Zeitschrift fur Kirchengeschichte* LXVIII (1957), pp. 1f.

Barnard, L. W., "St Stephen and Alexandrian Christianity" in *NTS* 7 (1960–1), pp. 31 f.

Barthélemey, D., "Chainon Manquant de l'Histoire de la Septante" in *RB* 60 (1953), pp. 18 f.

Battifol, P., "L'Eucharistie dans la Didache" in RB 2 (1905), pp. 58 f.

Bietenhard, D., art. ὀνομάζειν in TWNT.

Boismard, M. E., "Une Liturgie Baptismale dans la Prima Petri" in *RB* 63 (1956–7), pp. 182 f and 64 (1957), pp. 161 f.

Bornemann, W., "Der erste Petrusbrief—eine Taufrede des Silvanus?" in ZNTW 19 (1919–20), pp. 143 f.

Butler, B. C., "Two Ways in the Didache" in *JTS* 12 (1961), pp. 27 f.

Cullmann, O., "L'Opposition contre le Temple de Jerusalem etc." in *NTS* 5 (1958–9), pp. 157 f.

Dibelius, M., "Die Mahl-Gebete der Didache" in *ZNTW* 37 (1938), pp. 32 f.

Drews, P., "Untersuchungen zur Didache" in *ZNTW* 5 (1904), pp. 53 f.

Falconer, R., "I Timothy 2.14–15: Interpretative Notes" in *JBL* 60 (1941), p. 375.

Filson, F. V., "How much of the New Testament is Poetry?" in *JBL* 67 (1948), pp. 125 f.

Fitzer, G., art. σφράγις in TWNT.

Foakes-Jackson, F. J., "Stephen's Speech" in *JBL* 49 (1930), p. 283.

Foerster, W., "Εὐσεβεία in den Pastoralbriefen" in *NTS* 5 (1958–9), pp. 213 f.

Galtier, P., "La Reconciliation des Pécheurs dans la Première Épitre à Timothée" in *RSR* 39 (1951), pp. 317 f.

Gibbins, H. J., "The Problem of the Liturgical Section of the Didache" in *JTS* 35 (1935), pp. 373 f.

Glover, R., "The Didache's Quotations and the Synoptic Gospels" in *NTS* 5 (October 1958), pp. 12 f.

Hanson, R. P. C., "Studies in Texts: Acts 6.13" in *Theology* 51 (April 1947), p. 142.

Harrison, P. N., "The Authorship of the Pastoral Epistles" in *ET* 57 (1955–6), pp. 77 f.

Higgins, A. J. B., art. on "Pastoral Epistles" in Peake's Comm. on the Bible (revised edn, London 1962).

Hort, F. J. A., ἑδραίωμα in *ET* 8 (July 1897), p. 471.

Jeremias, J., art. ἀκρογωνιαῖος in *TWNT*.

Leaney, A. R. C., "I Peter and the Passover" in *NTS* 10 (1963–4), pp. 238 f.

McKelvey, R. J., "Christ the Cornerstone" in *NTS* 8 (July 1962), pp. 352 f.

Manson, T. W., Review art. of E. G. Selwyn's "I Peter" in *JTS*, 46 (1946), p. 220.

Marty, J., "Études des Textes cultuels du prière conservés par les pères apostoliques" in *RHPR* 10 (1930), pp. 90 f.

Michel, O., art. ὁμολογουμένως in *TWNT*.

Mitton, C. L., "The Relationship between I Peter and Ephesians" in *JTS* 1 (NS) (1950), pp 67 f.

Morris, L., "The Use of ἱλάσκεσθαι etc. in Biblical Greek" in *ET* 62 (May 1951), pp. 227 f.

Moule, C. F. D., "A Note on Didache 9.5" in *JTS* 6 (NS) (1955), pp. 240 f.

―― "The Nature and Purpose of I Peter" in *NTS* 13 (1956–7), pp. 1 f.

Murphy-O'Connor, J, "La 'Verité' chez Saint Paul et à Qumran" in *RB* 72 (1965), pp. 29–76.

Odeburg, H., art. Ἰαννῆς καὶ Ἰαμβρῆς in *TWNT*.

Oepke, A., art. μεσίτης in *TWNT*.

Peterson, E., "Didache cap. 9 e 10" in *Ephemerides Liturgicae* (January-December 1944), pp. 3 f.

Riesenfeld, H., "Das Brot von den Bergen" in *Eranos* 54 (1957), pp. 142 f.

Schneider, J., art. παράβασις in *TWNT*.

Schrenk, D. G., art γραφή in *TWNT*.

Schweizer, E., art. θεόπνευστος in *TWNT*.

Simon, M., "Saint Stephen and the Jerusalem Temple" in *Journal of Ecclesiastical History* 2 (1951), pp. 127 f.

Thackeray, H. St. J., "New Light on the Book of Jashar" in *JTS* 11 (1910), pp. 518 f.

Thornton, T. C. G., "I Peter, a Paschal Liturgy?" in *JTS* 12 (NS) (1961), pp. 14 f.

Van Unnik, W. C., "I Clement 34 and the Sanctus" in *Vigiliae Christianae* 5 (1951), pp. 204 f.

Wagner, G., "La Tabernacle et la Vie en Christ" in *RHPR* 41 (1961), pp. 379 f.

Windisch, H., "Zur Christologie der Pastoralbriefe" in *ZNTW* 34 (1935), pp. 213 f.

Index of References

(I wish to acknowledge the help of my son Philip Hanson in compiling this Index)

OLD TESTAMENT

QUMRAN DOCUMENTS

NEW TESTAMENT

PATRISTIC

THE BABYLONIAN TALMUD

(References are to the pages in the Soncino edition of the Babylonian Talmud in English)

Index of Names